Every Heart Tells

BY: NANCY RUSSO WILSON

I LOVE YOU ❤

the Peppertree Press
www.peppertreepublishing.com

ISBN: 978-1-61493-868-2
Library of Congress: 2022951662
Printed: January 2023
Manufactured in the United State of America

All photography and artwork by Nancy Russo Wilson

Dedication

To Bruce,
Always and forever and even longer than that!

Dearest Caroline,
Enjoy! God Bless
love, Nancy ☺

Other published works by author Nancy Russo Wilson:

The Princess Fish, The Gold Locket and the Air-World Kids

Hope Speaks and Love Listens

My Patients and me

How Does Truth Travel, Stories, Poems and Essays

Table of Contents

Introduction

I love words, I love puzzles. I love touching and holding things. I love to write, to tell stories and to listen to stories, I love to read. I love to observe and investigate things, people, and places.

I am the perfect crossword person, the perfect jigsaw puzzle person, the perfect … well, I am not sure. But I would love to be the perfect writer person for you at this moment.

I am happy in quiet places. Anyone who likes puzzles, reading, and writing is drawn to the quiet.

This book of essays started many years ago as my life came into being. My experiences may connect with your story. My searches for answers, clues, and connections in this life may mirror your searches.

I have spent my life in the service of others. I have learned how amazingly complex human life is. I know a few certain truths: what healing is, what matters to us as humans, what lessons we learn from nature and history.

I really don't *know* anything, actually, except one thing, I do know love. I do know that love connects the pieces, finishes the sentence, and tells the story—the rest? The mysteries? I'm clueless.

Well, that's why I love puzzles.

I hope you find your own story, your own connections and mysteries.

♥

CHAPTER 1

God Is in the Sky

Clouds and Rainbows

I lay on my back in the bow seat of our motorboat, the high clouds above me. It is a perfect summer day on Cayuga Lake in upstate New York.

The Clouds form fine filigreed curves, parabolas, and sweeping graceful shapes. They are changing constantly and are softly defined by the currents of the wind.

These are the very high clouds of summer. They are miles high up into a cerulean blue and deep azure sky. There are no sweet little popcorn puffs today—instead the clouds are huge, elegant and distant creatures, moving and in flight.

As I lay there, my arms begin to move above me, my hands forming little waving fluttering gestures. Each hand starts to trace a cloud-edge, not in harmony with the other hand.

Both arms and hands in motion, left moving down and up tracing a long-fingered corridor, right moving in rhythmic ovals and horizontal circles, hovering over another formation nearby. I began to smile.

My arms in orchestration move and flow, dance and hover around these shapes and as the boat keeps moving forward, I can't linger more than a few seconds before I must move on to the next measure, the next rhythm.

I am like a conductor waving two batons in a sweet elegant symphony of dancing whirls, sweeps and quiet caresses.

The silent sky, the bluest of backgrounds, the silent powerful winds aloft come down to me from the heavens, like a Greek God of Motion entering a simple human heart.

Mystery, life and movement come into my life and I am totally at one with the sky.

I have always loved clouds, and rainbows have always intrigued and delighted me. I must certainly have an ancient soul because I think of clouds like a mystic would.

I always look up at the sky when I am walking. I know the clouds are watching over me. I feel God in the Old and New Testaments.

A Navajo saying reads, "Send out your cloud towers to live with us. Stretch out your watery hands of mist. Let us embrace one another."

The Ancient Greeks, Celts, and Native tribes throughout time in every part of the world worshipped the meaning and symbolism of clouds.

For me, clouds have always just been there, always delighting me, and showing me the refuge of natural spaces.

I look up at the sky, wherever I am, and feel like I am facing a parallel universe, a true North, and I learn something.

Clouds are not a puzzle to me like time or love is. Clouds are a script for me to learn, relearn and remember every single time. I'm a cloud-watcher, but also feel that I once lived up there, lived as a being, a living yet eternal being. I feel I fell to earth and landed as a human being when I arose out of water. The lake? The ocean? I can't explain this.

I've always known something about the great mysteries of our being here. Even as a child I would sit for hours gazing at the sky.

Only later in life as I read ancient writings, tribal and Greek works, poets and scientists reaffirmed what I know. I'm not scientific about clouds—I just know them.

Late one day in Florida as I walked the Gulf Coast beach, I saw huge white-gray clouds and a rainbow after a brief rainstorm.

The rainbow astonished me. Appearing in the eastern sky at the same time as the storm was passing into the western sky and the sun was beginning to set. Orange on the west over a blue sea, and seven colors of God in the east. The orange, blue, indigo, violet, red, yellow and green colors of the arc were like a necklace or a tiara against a white mountain of clouds.

I stood still, in reverence and awe. I was watching a transformation. A white and glistening cloud was holding the rainbow in its arms and saying to me, "Look, here is my gift. Behold the beauty of God and life. We are vast and eternal, this rainbow and me, and into us you must fly."

On the western horizon, the sun was just setting over the water. There were a few clouds scattering around the blue sky. One was like a prancing stallion, another looked like a huge spaceship, while a third like a big poodle. All were moving through a slow shimmering sea mist.

I felt blessed and cleansed, humbled and instructed. I smiled to myself thinking, "Some truths are eternal."

There are many references to clouds over thousands of years. I've only known a few, which I've included here. One, a poem, "The Cloud" by Percy Bysshe Shelby, a second to a reference to a Wikipedia entry under "Rainbow."

I've also gathered some passages from the Old and New Testaments and will list them below. I hope you can experience joy and reflection and gain a certain comfort of wisdom to help you understand the sky above you.

Exodus 14:19-20

Exodus 33: 9-12

Luke 9:34

Luke 22:27

Ecclesiastes 24:4, 9, 50:7

Acts 1:9

Kings 8:10-13

Matthew 24:27

Revelation 1:7

Genesis 9:12-17

Nehemiah 9:12-13

The Cloud

BY PERCY BYSSHE SHELLEY

I bring fresh showers for the thirsting flowers,
From the seas and the streams;
I bear light shade for the leaves when laid
In their noonday dreams.
From my wings are shaken the dews that waken
The sweet buds every one,
When rocked to rest on their mother's breast,
As she dances about the sun.
I wield the flail of the lashing hail,
And whiten the green plains under,
And then again I dissolve it in rain,
And laugh as I pass in thunder.

I sift the snow on the mountains below,
And their great pines groan aghast;
And all the night 'tis my pillow white,
While I sleep in the arms of the blast.
Sublime on the towers of my skiey bowers,
Lightning my pilot sits;
In a cavern under is fettered the thunder,
It struggles and howls at fits;
Over earth and ocean, with gentle motion,
This pilot is guiding me,
Lured by the love of the genii that move
In the depths of the purple sea;
Over the rills, and the crags, and the hills,
Over the lakes and the plains,
Wherever he dream, under mountain or stream,
The Spirit he loves remains;
And I all the while bask in Heaven's blue smile,
Whilst he is dissolving in rains.

The sanguine Sunrise, with his meteor eyes,
And his burning plumes outspread,
Leaps on the back of my sailing rack,
When the morning star shines dead;
As on the jag of a mountain crag,
Which an earthquake rocks and swings,
An eagle alit one moment may sit
In the light of its golden wings.
And when Sunset may breathe, from the lit sea beneath,
Its ardours of rest and of love,
And the crimson pall of eve may fall
From the depth of Heaven above,
With wings folded I rest, on mine aëry nest,
As still as a brooding dove.

That orbèd maiden with white fire laden,
Whom mortals call the Moon,
Glides glimmering o'er my fleece-like floor,
By the midnight breezes strewn;
And wherever the beat of her unseen feet,
Which only the angels hear,
May have broken the woof of my tent's thin roof,
The stars peep behind her and peer;
And I laugh to see them whirl and flee,
Like a swarm of golden bees,
When I widen the rent in my wind-built tent,
Till calm the rivers, lakes, and seas,
Like strips of the sky fallen through me on high,
Are each paved with the moon and these.

I bind the Sun's throne with a burning zone,
And the Moon's with a girdle of pearl;
The volcanoes are dim, and the stars reel and swim,
When the whirlwinds my banner unfurl.
From cape to cape, with a bridge-like shape,
Over a torrent sea,
Sunbeam-proof, I hang like a roof,
The mountains its columns be.
The triumphal arch through which I march
With hurricane, fire, and snow,
When the Powers of the air are chained to my chair,
Is the million-coloured bow;
The sphere-fire above its soft colours wove,
While the moist Earth was laughing below.

I am the daughter of Earth and Water,
And the nursling of the Sky;
I pass through the pores of the ocean and shores;
I change, but I cannot die.
For after the rain when with never a stain
The pavilion of Heaven is bare,
And the winds and sunbeams with their convex gleams
Build up the blue dome of air,
I silently laugh at my own cenotaph,
And out of the caverns of rain,
Like a child from the womb, like a ghost from the tomb,
I arise and unbuild it again.

Rainbows

From Wikipedia, the free encyclopedia

A **rainbow** is an optical and meteorological phenomenon that is caused by both reflection and refraction of light in water droplets resulting in a spectrum of light appearing in the sky. It takes the form of a multicoloured arc. Rainbows caused by sunlight always appear in the section of sky directly opposite the sun.

Rainbows can be full circles, however, the average observer sees only an arc, formed by illuminated droplets above the ground, and centred on a line from the sun to the observer's eye.

In a "primary rainbow", the arc shows red on the outer part and violet on the inner side. This rainbow is caused by light being refracted (bent) when entering a droplet of water, then reflected inside on the back of the droplet and refracted again when leaving it.

In a double rainbow, a second arc is seen outside the primary arc, and has the order of its colours reversed, red facing toward the other one, in both rainbows. This second rainbow is caused by light reflecting twice inside water droplets.

Overview

The rainbow is not located at a specific distance, but comes from an optical illusion caused by any water droplets viewed from a certain angle relative to a light source. Thus, a rainbow is not an object and cannot be physically approached. Indeed, it is impossible for an observer to see a rainbow from water droplets at any angle other than the customary one of 42 degrees from the direction opposite the light source. Even if an observer sees another observer who seems "under" or "at the end of" a rainbow, the second observer will see a different rainbow—farther off—at the same angle as seen by the first observer.

A rainbow spans a continuous spectrum of colours. Any distinct bands perceived are an artefact of human colour vision, and no banding of any type is seen in a black-and-white photo of a rainbow, only a smooth gradation of intensity to a maximum, then fading towards the other side. For colours seen by the human eye, the most commonly cited and remembered sequence is Newton's sevenfold red, orange, yellow, green, blue, indigo and violet.

Rainbows can be caused by many forms of airborne water. These include not only rain, but also mist, spray, and airborne dew.

Visibility

Rainbows can be observed whenever there are water drops in the air and sunlight shining from behind at a low altitude angle. The most spectacular rainbow displays happen when half the sky is still dark with raining clouds and the observer is at a spot with clear sky in the direction of the sun. The result is a luminous rainbow that contrasts with the darkened background.

The rainbow effect is also commonly seen near waterfalls or fountains. In addition, the effect can be artificially created by dispersing water droplets into the air during a sunny day. Rarely, a moonbow, lunar rainbow or nighttime rainbow, can be seen on strongly moonlit nights. As human visual perception for colour is poor in low light, moonbows are often perceived to be white.

It is difficult to photograph the complete semicircle of a rainbow in one frame, as this would require an angle of view of 84. For a 35 mm camera, a lens with a focal length of 19 mm or less wide-angle lens would be required. Now that powerful software for stitching several images into a panorama is available, images of the entire arc and even secondary arcs can be created fairly easily from a series of overlapping frames. From an aeroplane, one has the opportunity to see the whole circle of the rainbow, with the plane's shadow in the centre. This phenomenon can be confused with the glory, but a glory is usually much smaller, covering only 5–20.

At good visibility conditions (for example, a dark cloud behind the rainbow), the second arc can be seen, with inverse order of colours. At the background of the blue sky, the second arc is barely visible.

As is evident by the photos on this page, the sky inside of a primary rainbow is brighter than the sky outside of the bow. This is because each raindrop is a sphere and it scatters light in a many-layered stack of coloured discs over an entire circular disc in the sky, but only the edge of the disc, which is coloured, is what is called a rainbow. Alistair Fraser, coauthor of *The Rainbow Bridge: Rainbows in Art, Myth, and Science*, explains: "Each color has a slightly different-sized disc and since they overlap except for the edge, the overlapping colors give white, which brightens the sky on the inside of the circle. On the edge, however, the different-sized colored discs don't overlap and display their respective colors—a rainbow arc."

Light of primary rainbow arc is 96% polarized tangential to the arch. Light of second arc is 90% polarized.

Number of colours in spectrum or rainbow

A spectrum obtained using a glass prism and a point source is a continuum of wavelengths without bands. The number of colours that the human eye is able to distinguish in a spectrum is in the order of 100. Accordingly, the Munsell colour system (a 20th-century system for numerically describing colours, based on equal steps for human visual perception) distinguishes 100 hues. The apparent discreteness of main colours is an artefact of human perception and the exact number of main colours is a somewhat arbitrary choice.

Red	Orange	Yellow	Green	Blue	Indigo	Violet

Newton originally (1672) divided the spectrum into five main colours; red, yellow, green, blue and violet. Later he included orange and indigo, giving seven main colours by analogy to the number of notes in a musical scale. Newton chose to arbitrarily divide the visible spectrum into seven colours out of a belief, derived from the beliefs of the ancient Greek sophists, who thought there was a connection between the colours, the musical notes, the known objects in the Solar System, and the days of the week.

According to Isaac Asimov, "It is customary to list indigo as a color lying between blue and violet, but it has never seemed to me that indigo is worth the dignity of being considered a separate color. To my eyes it seems merely deep blue." Others suggest that Newton in fact called "indigo" the colour now called "blue", and "blue" the colour now called "cyan" (see Indigo# Classification as a spectral color).

The colour pattern of a rainbow is different from a spectrum, and the colours are less saturated. There is spectral smearing in a rainbow owing to the fact that for any particular wavelength, there is a distribution of exit angles, rather than a single unvarying angle. In addition, a rainbow is a blurred version of the bow obtained from a point source, because the disk diameter of the sun (0.5°) cannot be neglected compared to the width of a rainbow (2°). The number of colour bands of a rainbow may therefore be different from the number of bands in a spectrum, especially if the droplets are either large or small. Therefore, the number of colours of a rainbow is variable. If, however, the word *rainbow* is used inaccurately to mean *spectrum*, it is the number of main colours in the spectrum.

CHAPTER 2

Every Heart Tells a Story

Ho - ly, ho - ly, ho- ly, my heart, my heart a-dores you!

Prepared by Digital Songs and Hymns, LLC, 2006

My heart pours out my praise to_ you; you are ho - ly, Lord.

Prepared by Digital Songs and Hymns, LLC, 2006

The Santo - "The Heart"
An Argentine
Chant

*O*ur church offers a preschool, where the children are young, playful and energetic. They play all sorts of games and the classrooms are full of books and toys, games, drawings and posters.

Their little chairs and stools sit in teaching circles. After the children are seated, the teachers sit right down among them. During recess, the children laugh and occasionally shriek playfully as they run and scramble with amazing energy on the playground swings, slides and climbing toys. It is a joy to be around them.

The one time in the week the classrooms are quieter is when the teacher cuts out paper hearts and writes the prayer each child is telling her. The paper hearts, all in wonderful colorful pink, yellow, blue, orange, green, and reds are then placed into a basket that sits on the altar every Sunday. Before communion and after the prayer of the people, the priest reads these "heart prayers" aloud.

With each prayer, the reactions among us (the older ones, the elders, the ones with life more behind us than before us) to the sweet and often simple, profound calls from the hearts of these young beings range from "Ah, how sweet!" to "Oh no! Poor child," to "Wow! What are these children dealing with in their lives?"

Each paper heart tells a story. Here is a collection from several services. As you read them, I hope the hidden story, the truth and the sweetness of these innocent children will teach and inspire you. Their insights are ageless. Their prayers are in all our hearts.

As I sat here and read and wrote down each prayer heart, I was struck by several truths:

- These children are not even seven years old. Yet their prayers tell me they worry about their parents' health and well-being.
- These prayers show me they are very aware of their own needs for connection with their parents. Their prayers show gratitude for friends, school teachers, school friends, pets, and grandparents.
- They are genuine reflections of the realities of these young lives.

Yes, they are in school and yes, they have teachers, a parent, maybe a grandparent, or both parents, or siblings. But their prayers show me they already know the answers. They already know they have to speak to a power greater than themselves so their story can be heard.

Every Heart Tells a Story

After the Prayers of the People, the priest reads the "heart-prayers" aloud.

With each prayer, the reactions among us, (the older ones, the elders?, the ones with life more behind us than before us) to the sweet and often simple, profound calls from the hearts of these young beings range from "ahs, how sweet!" to "oh no! poor child", to "wow! what are these children dealing with in their lives?"

Each paper heart tells a story. Here is a collection from several services. As you read them, the hidden story, the truth and the sweetness of these innocent children will teach you and will inspire you in their insights are ageless. Their prayers are in all of our hearts.

A
STORY

I WANT TO PRAY for MY UNCLES DOG. He DIED.

THANK YOU FOR MY MOMMY, GOD

I WANT TO PRAY FOR MY FAMILY. I AM HAPPY WITH THEM.

MOMMY AND DADDY TO PLAY WITH ME MORE

HELP DADDY GET NEW TIRES FOR HIS BIKE

MOMMY AND DADDY TO SLEEP WITH ME AND HELP ME NOT BE AFRAID OF THE DARK

Thank you FOR MY SCHOOL

I LOVE GOD AND HE LOVES ME AND I AM GOING TO BRING HIM CEREAL.

I WOULD LIKE TO PRAY FOR MY DOG. SHE IS SO CUTE.

I WANT MOMMY AND DADDY TO HAVE A FUN DAY. MY SISSY TOO.

HI GOD, THANK YOU FOR THE BIRDS IN THE SKY.

THANK YOU FOR MY NEW FRIEND JULIANA.

I LOVE GOD, HE TAKES CARE OF MY FAMILY.

DEAR GOD, LET MOMMY AND DADDY PLAY WITH ME MORE.

FOR HOPPY MY DOG TO NOT RUN AWAY

I AM THANKFUL FOR MY TOYS GOD

FOR MOMMY TO GET ME BACK

GOD,
HELP MY BROTHER,
HE WAS IN THE TIME-OUT CHAIR.

FOR PEACHES.
SHE HURT HER POOR LITTLE NOSE.

DEAR GOD,
THANK YOU FOR GRANDMA VICKY,
I LOVE HER.

FOR MOMMY,
I MISS HER GOD

I LOVE MY FAVORITE PAIR OF SOCKS.

FOR MOMMY AND DADDY TO HAVE A GOOD DAY AND TO PLAY WITH ME

FOR PAPA MARTY. HE IS IN WASHINGTON.

HELP MY FAMILY TO BE KIND TO EVERYONE.

FOR MY GRANDMA. SHE HURT HER FINGERS.

FOR THE WORLD AND THE FISH WITH PLASTIC AND THE ANIMALS PEOPLE KILL FOR FUR.

I WANT TO GO TO THE STORE.

I WANT TO THANK GOD FOR HELPING ME WITH HARD STUFF.

FOR MOMMY AND DADDY TO PLAY WITH ME MORE AND KNOW HOW MUCH I LOVE THEM

FOR MOMMY AND DADDY TO BE KIND TO MY FRIENDS

FOR MY MOMMY BECAUSE SHE IS MY GIRLFRIEND.

THANK YOU GOD FOR MY TOYS.

FOR MOMMY TO PLAY WITH ME AND GIVE ME HUGS.

I PRAY FOR MOMMY AND DADDY TO HAVE TWO BABIES.

I WANT TO PRAY FOR JACKSON. HE FELL OFF HIS BIKE.

I LOVE GOD BECAUSE HE IS HERE AT SCHOOL AND LOVES THE BABIES.

DADDY TO FEEL BETTER SO HE CAN PLAY WITH ME.

MAKE SURE THE KIDS ARE NOT TOO LOUD FOR PRINCESS BUTTERCUP, THE BUNNY.

THANK YOU FOR THE FIRE STATION.

I LOVE GOD.

FOR MY BROTHER'S FRIEND, SHE IS LEAVING TODAY FOR ANOTHER STATE.

I PRAY FOR MY BABY BROTHER.

I PRAY FOR MY DOG, HIS BARK IS SOFT.

FOR MY FRIEND LILY. I MISS HER.

FOR MY FRIEND JOSEPH SO HE CAN FEEL HAPPY.

FOR MOMMY TO GIVE ME A SISTER AND A BROTHER. DADDY TO PLAY WITH ME.

MY DADDY BECAUSE A CAR FELL ON HIS LEG.

HELP POP-POP DRIVE SAFE. WE ARE GOING TO A PICNIC. I LOVE PICNICS WITH MY FAMILY.

HELP MY FRIEND BRANTLEY HEAL HIS BOO-BOO UP.

DEAR GOD, I WANT MY DOG TO NEVER EVER GROWL EVEN WHEN I PULL HER TAIL.

FOR MOM AND DAD TO PLAY HOOPS WITH ME IN MY ROOM

I LOVE JESUS.

DEAR GOD, HELP DADDY GET US A NEW TABLE. IT GOT BROKEN LEGS.

I LOVE MY NANA. THANK YOU GOD.

MOMMY AND DADDY
TO HAVE A GOOD DAY
AND
TO GET A NEW
DOG.

I PRAY FOR
MY DADDY, HE
IS SICK.

HELP MY FRIEND
NORMA FEEL GOOD, SHE
HAS BEEN SICK A
LONG TIME.

I AM HAPPY TO
VISIT MS. CONNIES
HOUSE.

I WANT TO THANK
GOD FOR THE WHOLE
WORLD.

FOR MY SISTER
TO BE NICE
TO
ME

I WANT GOD TO
MAKE SURE MY
FAMILY
STAYS
SAFE.

THANK YOU FOR MY SCHOOL AND TEACHERS, I HAVE SO MUCH FUN.

MAKE MY BROTHER PHIL HAPPY. HE IS SAD BECAUSE MY BROTHER AARON WONT GO WATCH HIS BASKETBALL GAME.

MOMMY TO PUT MY TOYS AWAY AND PLAY WITH ME.

THANK YOU FOR BATHS.

MOMMY AND DADDY TO GET A NEW DOG AND BE SAFE ON THEIR TRIP.

I AM THANKFULL FOR MY FAMILY AND MY FRIENDS.

I AM EXCITED FOR MY MOM TO COME HOME.

FOR MY FRIENDS.
I LOVE THEM.

MAKE SURE MY MOM
GIVES ME MEDICINE
AT THE
RIGHT
TIME.

GOD LOVES ME.

MY MOM TOLD ME GOD
LOVES ME ALL THE
TIME.

PRAY FOR MY FISH.
I KNOW IF YOU FEED
THE FISH A LOT
IT DIES.

MAKE MY MOM FEEL
BETTER WHEN SHE
IS SICK.

MOMMY AND DADDY
TO HAVE A GOOD
DAY AND A
SAFE
TRIP.

THANK YOU FOR
MY FAMILY AND
MY
NANA.

MOMMY TO FEEL BETTER TODAY.

DADDY TO FEEL GOODER.

MOMMY NOT TO BE SICK.

DADDY'S ARM TO GET BETTER

MOMMY TO FEEL BETTER.

MOMMY AND DADDY TO BE GOOD.

DADDY TO FEEL BETTER.

MAKE MY MOM FEEL BETTER WHEN SHE IS SICK. SHE IS SICK ALOT.

CHAPTER 3

Aesop's Fables, Myths and Proverbs

Aesop's Fables, Myths, and Proverbs – How we Learn

*I*f there was one collection of words known to humans that would teach them life, wisdom, truth, how to live and how to learn, it would be the book, *Aesop's Fables*.

I wish every child, then teenager, then adult not only had access to these Fables, but was required to learn and relearn their wise, simple truths their whole lives long.

Tradition says that around 620 BC, a slave was born in the Middle-Eastern/Mediterranean. This slave was eventually given his freedom and his brilliant storytelling, wit and wisdom has been cherished during more than eighteen centuries!

Today we see and say his words, and teach his lessons and remind ourselves of his wisdom all the time.

Philosophers, orators, famous men from the ancient world, warriors, kings, simple peasants, children, and poets, all use the "genre" of the Fable to teach, govern, communicate, and connect with others.

Here are a few of his lessons. The last sentence carries the bang. The short Fable carries the story I'm sure you have read:

- Don't count your chickens before they hatch.
- He is a wolf in sheep's clothing.
- Necessity is the mother of invention.
- Persuasion is better than force.
- Misfortune tests the sincerity of friendship.
- Don't waste your pity on a scamp.
- Evil wishes, like fowls, come home to roost.
- You cannot believe a liar even when he tells the truth.
- You may play a good card once too often.
- Look before you leap.
- Deeds, not words.
- Show gratitude where gratitude is due.
- Union is strength.

There are hundreds more. Go buy the book *of Aesop's Fables*, you will love it.

Myths

- Thousands of years before Aesop, ancient civilizations used myths to teach, govern and guide early human life and behavior. Myths were early science, justice, and religion.
- In Asia, India, Africa, Meso and Latin America, in Native Indian lands from Alaska to Russia, peoples "wrote" stories on pieces of rock, or parchment using symbols, basic forms, caricatures of animals,

the sun, the moon, the planets, and the oceans. Most myths were oral, and brought into the light through centuries of experience around campfires, in deep incense-filled caves or in stone temples.

- In ancient Greece the word, chreia, meant a brief useful anecdote about a person.

- In Zen practice, again from ancient beginnings, the koan was a story, a dialogue, a statement of deep spiritual truths.

- The ancient people of the Indian continent told their tales in Jataka and Panchatantra stories.

- In early European cultures, maxims relayed general truths or principles.

- As humans developed their storytelling, proverbs arose, short pithy sayings that stated a general truth, a piece of advice, or like in the Christian faiths, moral teachings or canons.

- Fables, like Aesop's, often used animals and people known in cultures, such as farmers, hunters, travelers, ruler, and the like, so when that last moral was conveyed at the end of the short tale, it was universally recognized.

- The simple yet profound truths of these centuries-old means of teaching humans how to live are actually very sophisticated.

- Why are myths, legends, fables, and proverbs actually brilliant and everlasting through thousands of years? I believe it is because through their use of allegory, patterns, and connections, and through their remarkable insights into human behavior, they capture the very essence of human existence.

    - Let me develop this for you. Let's start with an allegory, which is a story or truth being taught. An allegory has several layers of meaning, so it has depth, because its innermost lesson is often hidden, profound and available only to those who can see hidden meanings and truths. These truths are not obvious. You can read a story for its appearance outwardly but inwardly, there is deep, richer meaning.

        - Allegories are adaptable and can put new thoughts into older patterns. Because of this feature, they can connect things in a very sophisticated, yet humble way.

        - So, a fable or a myth, koan, chreia, proverb, or a moral can on the surface just be a story to read to a child. Dig a little deeper and it can teach an adult, then put the wisdom into action, and perhaps win a battle for a leader.

        - Fables look for patterns and repetitions and for a moral life. Like proverbs, which use keen observation, ethics and piety, these ancient human stories can persuade, amuse, foster unity and uncover the worst of human behaviors, thus their brilliance endures to this day.

- So, what about today? In the twenty-first century, how do we learn? How do we tell our stories, teach ourselves and others how to know truths, wisdoms, deeper meanings and connections? We still use the simple truths.

- I have always believed that humans and human nature are unchanged from the first moments of creation. We are social creatures, having basic needs, tribal and competitive, and we have enormous capacity for love and connection. We also have that same capacity for hatred and violence.

- We learn the hard way—experience. We learn when lessons are short and rich and we can take the meaning, the "lesson" on many levels. We can learn something as a quick reminder or we can ponder a wise statement that encourages deeper thought. Through familiar images and sights, social media, and through one to five word replies on Twitter to quiet thoughts in a private space, we learn what is going on in the world around us. Human beings are naïve and sophisticated at the same time. We tend to strive for outward symbols of wealth, acceptance and success, so we join groups to stay connected and to stay safe within our realm, be it our family, our classmates, or co-workers, or any group we join.

- Some humans want to be seen, others to be hidden. Some modern humans know that free speech, writing, and religion comes with a price.
- The price some humans pay for telling their stories, writing their myths and legends, and living out their concept of life is that they may be scorned or attacked or perhaps just ignored by others.
- There is truth and there are facts. In today's world, someone can write or say something on social media and can actually make a huge personal and financial profit, but what they are saying could be false.
- Unlike ancient times, when humans took the truths, morals, and the lessons of proverbs, allegories, or myths, and accepted their wisdoms, today's humans have embraced technology as their teacher, social media as their guiding light.
- Technology is brilliant—we have created devices and discovered through science an invention of incredible things. I'm concerned that in the 21st century our visions of humanity don't actually recognize the deeper truth of human existence that our ancient ancestors, indeed our own DNA as a species, knew and require.

We require learning and acceptance of basic needs for survival, but we also require and often ignore our species' need for connection. We are a curious species, thus our love of mysteries, puzzles, games, and the unknown. We strive to learn, to be taught, to be led, to be saved, to be loved and to live in community with others. Rebels, mothers, teachers, coaches, politicians, fathers, doctors, mates … we need each other to learn from the stories and legends of millennia.

CHAPTER 4

Prayer

Part 1

What is prayer? I have many more questions than answers. Prayer, the quiet grace I feel when I'm focused, has been at the core of my life for as long as I can remember.

I always felt an urge to speak to God even as a child, and even when I didn't know who God was. I just knew there was something very mysterious, comforting, illuminating and beckoning inside of me. And I came to know the Divine Force of Life. I call Him, God, through my child's heart.

I was a rebel in Catholic School, which lasted to the second grade. My parents were my first teachers of the truths of holiness. They taught me to be gentle and joyful. They showed me how to be courteous, patient and modest. They taught me that God is Love.

As I grew and lived my life in various stages, I always had a desire to help others. From wanting to be a nun as a young girl, I chose to express my devotional instincts as I trained to be a teacher and a nurse. My entire life has been lived in the service of others. I knew that my instincts to be a caregiver came from a holy source both within and outside of me.

I have read hundreds of books and articles on prayer, faith, religion, the lives of saints, the teachings of Greeks, Native peoples, the wisdom of Confucius and the Sacred texts of the Hebrews, the Catholics, and the Buddhists.

From all those sources I learned a few basic truths. I can't prove any of them. I just know them.

I'm going to write down some thoughts I've had over the years, and then I will give you sayings, themes and writings of others over the centuries. I will also share with you my favorite prayers. I will end by giving you two prayers I wrote and say almost every day.

We all come from different places. I would never expect my life's thoughts and experiences to be yours. To clarify: I use the word, "God" to mean the great divine Life-force of this universe. I will not place religion in the same discussion as faith and prayer, for they are different things. Prayer is the way we can talk to, ask for help from, give thanks to, and express Love to this Divine Force. You will have your own words as you pray. Here are some of my thoughts on prayer and faith:

- God needs only two things from me—my simple heart and my belief in him.
- You must first find your heart, then you can develop your faith.
- Thank God for who you are and pray to him to free you from yourself.
- God is a patient teacher. He teaches truth and truth preceded human life.
- Be gentle, be joyful and love people.
- God is Spirit and your spirit is His, not your body nor your emotions.
- We show ourselves to our fellow humans in one way and to God in another way.
- Is there any possibility of happiness without faith?
- Extreme piety can be destructive.
- Humility is a necessity for saintliness.

- When we hear a voice inside us that isn't ours, it is God showing us a brief moment of clarity (I call that truth).

- Sometimes we end up in a place we didn't choose, and are led by a way we can't understand. Follow your instincts, even if you are clueless. You might see that flicker of grace, which is always in us.

- Is faith more powerful than fear? Wouldn't it be amazing to be able to combine them?

- I have a hunger for God.

- All you have to do to have God in your life is to ask Him and accept Him. Stay closer to your prayer-life and you will stay soft.

- Everyone needs hope

- Logic gives factual results. Faith gives mystery.

- "Dear Nancy,

    Thanks you for your offer to help but I think I can do this myself."

                                                    Cordially, God

- Pay attention to the world around you. Be silent, look and listen. Seek quiet places where you can listen to God's voice. You must be quiet to hear.

- When you pray, your mind opens a door to your soul and your soul sees the "Beyond."

- Meditation and mindfulness require quiet because the Soul often whispers.

- Our lives are so brief, it is ridiculous to assume we are immortal. The only true purpose for using our bodies and our minds, our actions, our spirits and our love is to express truth and wisdom, so we hopefully can see and feel the life beyond this one.

- Is prayer loud or soft? Do I use words or music or dance? Do I sing with a bird above me, do I pray through a cloud to the life beyond it?

- Native peoples knew their prayers were known to Nature's Spirit. They saw and felt the signs of Love in the wind, the sky, the water, the stones and fire and were grateful.

- God keeps me company. I feel his voice in me. If I'm sad or lonely, he listens and reassures me.

- When I was seeking "the mysteries," I would walk the beach. I would look at nature. I would have a true hunger for God.

- One day I was in a taxicab in New York City. The driver was a Muslim, turbaned and soft-spoken. We started a conversation about God. I told him I was seeking the mysteries, that I wanted them to be revealed to me and that I would keep praying to be an angel. He looked at me in his rearview mirror, soft brown eyes, and said quietly, "You are close to being an angel and you will grow into it." I will never forget that conversation. I hope he is right.

- Breathing in deeply is my "Hello" to God. Smiling is my "Hello" to myself. All in one.

- Pray with all five senses.

- God comes to us suddenly, sometimes in thoughts or sensations. Hold them until they leave you.

- Humility is critical for faith.

- Pure prayer lights up our intellects.

- The spiritual affects the physical. The physical affects the spiritual.

- Love and self-control purify our souls.

- Find a space where you can just "be" in the moment. Commune with the voice and spirit of the Maker.

Part 2

I have read many books about holy people, saints, mystics, poets, spiritual leaders, and ordinary people who accomplished extraordinary things. Some of the following quotations are anonymous, others are attributed to real people. As I read them today, writing them for you, I try to imagine where they were when they wrote or said these things. Were they on a mountaintop or in a small monistic room? Were they in the middle of a city or amidst fellow villagers? The actions and lives of holy people amaze me. They show me that prayer, through love and grace, is the single most powerful force in human existence.

- "There is a light within a person of light and it shines on the whole world."

> *#24 Gospel of Thomas*

- "Divine sparks of light enlighten the life of a person of knowledge."

> *Gospel of Thomas*

- "Let nothing trouble you. Let nothing frighten you. All things pass away. God never changes. Patience obtains all things. Nothing is lacking to me who possesses God. God alone suffices.

> *St. Teresa of Avila*

Prayers

"Lord, make me an instrument of thy Peace.

Where there is hatred, let me sow love.

Where there is injury; pardon.

Where there is doubt; faith.

Where there is despair; hope.

Where there is darkness; light, and

Where there is sadness; joy.

Oh, Divine Master, grant that I may not so much seek to be consoled as to console; to be understood as to understand; to be loved as to love;

For it is in the giving that we receive, It is in the pardoning that we are pardoned and it is in the dying that we are born to eternal Life."

> *St. Francis of Assisi*

"Joy springs from purity of heart and constant prayer. It is our lot in life to be happy."

> *St. Francis of Assisi*

"I have held many things in my hands and I have lost them all; but whatever I have placed in God's hands, that I still possess."

> *Martin Luther*

"The ten gifts of Love are love, joy, patience, humility, kindness, faithfulness, generosity, gentleness, peace, self-control."

> *St. Paul to the Galations*

"If the only prayer you ever say is 'Thank You,' it is enough."

Meister Eckhardt

"Together met, forever bound we go our separate ways."

Unknown, possibly Brian Wren

"Fear shows an absence of faith."

Unknown

"Nothing is as it seems. At any minute reality can switch and change into something else and we are not in control."

Unknown

"Little by little we must advance on the road to prayer. The technique is always the same. Clear the heart of surrounding distraction, to yield to what our hearts are telling us until the Spirit's prayer becomes our own."

Father Andre Loub, Abbot
Cistercian Monastery
Mont-des-Cat, France

"Happy is he who has knowledge that comes from seeing deathless nature, of what it is made, whence, how, and the Force which made it."

Europedes, Greek poet
485 BC

"Death is mightier than all but charity (Zedakah). Deeds of charity save from Death!"

Proverbs 10:2
Rabbi Judah Talmud

"One man is worth an entire nation, if he is wise. There are many religions and ways to worship God—all you need is to love, let Him know he is remembered."

Maximus of Tyre
2nd CCE

"God, I am bathing my face in the nine rays of the sun, as Mary bathed her son in generous milk fermented.

"Sweetness – be in my face; Riches – be in my countenance, comb-honey- be in my tongue, my breath as the incense.

"Black is yonder house, blacker men therein. I am the White Swan, queen over them. I will go in the name of God, in likeness of deer, of horse, of serpent, of king, victorious in God's praise."

Ancient Celtic Prayer
Carmina Gadelica

"If you brought life to many lives and made connections in your life, you will be on top of the cone of light, where most light reaches. Beams of light connecting in this life will connect again in the afterlife. We are bodies of Light, travelling through Time and Space, spanning worlds externally connected to one another and to the Higher Force."

Islamic quote

"The Great Spirit, the Sacred Divine, the great mystery is called 'Wakan Tanka.' He is in the animals, the clouds, the flowers, our foods, plants and vegetables. He is in Music. He is in Nature.

The Life forms of the Entire Universe is a system of relationships with humans who get their power and meaning and identity from those relationships.

Prayer invokes those relationships. We use the morning star as our wisdom. We lie in our sacred hoop of the earth, the sky, the water, the wind, the sun and moon."

North American Lakota Indian Creed

"It is from understanding that power comes; to be wise and follow your vision in this world of shadows and darkness, to pray to what is true and beautiful, and to raise your thoughts as high as eagles. To be holy, to sing the sun as it rises."

Black Elk,
Sioux holy man

"That which I am and all that I am with my gifts of Nature and Grace, You have given me.
And you are Lord of all this.
I offer this all to you, principally to serve you and praise you and to help my fellow man and myself and to keep the faith."

The Cloud of Unknowing

"Behold, my sister, the true image of womanhood and remember yourself in God. Embrace your holy soul and the sacredness of your womanhood."

Mary Magdalene

"The Power of Prayer is Silence."

Unknown

"The greater healing is not in the body. It is beyond the body."

Unknown

"Do not fear death or dying. It is merely the passage into new Life."

Unknown

"Look to see what is hidden and you will understand. Truth is hidden by the visible."

Unknown

"Pondus Meum Amor Meus.
My Love to my weight. Where it goes I go."

Saint Augustine

"God, grant me the Serenity to accept the things I cannot change; the courage to change the things I can and the wisdom to know the difference."

The Serenity Prayer AA

"The three-fold flame of Sophia is faith, hope and love, but invariably it is knowledge, understanding and wisdom. Ask God for this holy flame."

St. Mary Magdalene
(Malachi)

"Envision a spiritual sun shining in your heart and gather yourself into it. Let go of surface consciousness, tension, and negativity. Identify yourself with the 'Light-Presence' in you. Go into your heart and abide in the Light."

St. Mary Magdalene
(Malachi)

Part 3

What follows and concludes this section on prayer are prayers I have written. They were published in my book, *How Does Truth Travel*, so I definitely have the author's permission to use them here.

I deeply hope that in your life you can pray and find peace.

Defining Prayer

I've included some definitions and origins for word of prayer:

Prayer	Devout petition to God or an object of worship; spiritual communion, adoration or confession; a supplication; freely given love to God in grace.
Origin	Latin: Prayer – precarious; obtained by entreaty Latin: Supplication (supplicate) – to kneel Plicare – to bend, fold.
Grace	Favor, kindness: Gratus
Communion	Latin: Communis – com (duty) munus (task, duty gift)

Prayers

Memories are prayers, tears are prayers,
Smiles are prayers, touching and
Holding another human being is a prayer.

Nancy's Prayer

April 20, 2002

Dear God—give me wit and wisdom,
Patience and gentleness.
Let me know the nature of all things
And let me accept the nature of all things.

Keep my loved ones safe in the comfort of your loving arms.
Let your spirit flow through me
And let time pass gracefully—Amen

Prayer Mantra

Your hand to guide me,
Your meaning inside me,
My hands to work and pray for You,
My value is that I love You.
Woman, Your fire and stone,
Woman, who holds you in her arms?
If I cry, You inside me cry.
When I laugh, so do You.
If You are inside of me I cannot
Be full of anything other than You.
I cannot hate, I cannot despair,
I cannot weep, I cannot fear.
You need me, your value is in my love
For You. We are the same being,
Only, I am still unformed.
Waiting to become like You.
Show me the Mysteries.
I want to be an angel.
I love You.

A Conversation with God on the Beach

God: Where do you live now?

Woman: I live in the hearts of my friends and loved ones, in the graces and courtesies of my daily actions. I live in the sunshine, amongst the shore birds and flowers. I live in the water where I swim. I live in the abundance and blessings of the life you have given me here in Sarasota.

God: Where did you come from?

Woman: I come from the lakes and hills, green with high grasses and white with snow. I come from the woods and streams, the waterfalls and gorges and the sky where geese flew over in squawking squadrons. I come from the place where my mother and father, sister and brother lived and from my home where I made family dinners for all of us and we laughed together and the children played. I come from all the places I ever worked. I come from the memories and hearts of my friends and family in Ithaca, New York.

God: Why did you come here?

Woman: You told me I could, remember? I spoke to you every morning at the lakeshore. That is where I cried and prayed and waited. When you gave me permission I left all I had loved and known and came here to this beach, where we speak again to one another. Where do you come from?

God: From ancient places, epochs of eternity, from the darkness and space and light of all Life.

Woman: Where do you live now?

God: I live in the wind and the sea. I live in the sun's rays and the sparkle on the water. I live on the wings of the birds, in children's laughter and in the bones of old wise people. I live in everyone's heart.

Woman: Why did you come here?

God: I was lonely.

Woman: Come, let's walk beside the waves. Take my hand.

Breast Stroke Prayer

The breast stroke is a swimming stroke born for meditation. Head up, breathe, arms swing out then come together with hands as in purposeful forward gliding prayer. Then legs kicking into a forward glide, rest, begin again. I think it is the breathing which makes this the stroke I pray with.

Sometimes I am in a "prayer-zone" so intense I do not know how many breast stroke laps I have done and when I glance up at the clock I see minutes have passed and my body, soul and mind have been in a waterworld other-world rhythm.

This morning I prayed this:

Thank you God for the air and sun, the sea and sky, the moon and the stars. Thank you for flowers, thank you for trees, thank you for birds, thank you for sunsets and rainbows and horses and puppies. Thank you for mountains and rivers. Thank you for clouds. Thank you for snow and springtime blossoms. Thank you for time and space, for love and truth.

Thank you for my husband and family and our love for each other. Thank you for babies. Thanks you for Earth and mankind.

Thank you for forgiveness and redemption. Watch over us, we are fragile and lost.

Peace before

1. Peace before us, peace behind us,
2. Love before us, love behind us,
3. Light before us, light behind us,
4. Christ before us, Christ behind us,

peace under our feet. Peace within us,
love under our feet. Love within us,
light under our feet. Light within us,
Christ under our feet. Christ within us,

[1, 2, 3, 4, 5.]

peace over us, let all around us be peace.
love over us, let all around us be love.
light over us, let all around us be light.
Christ over us, let all around us be Christ.

[6.]

6. peace. Let all around us be peace.

6. Let all around us be peace.

5. Alleluia, alleluia, alleluia.
   Alleluia, alleluia, alleluia.
6. Peace before us, peace behind us,
   peace under our feet.
   Peace within us, peace over us,
   let all around us be peace. *(three times)*

Words: David Haas (b. 1957), based on a Navaho prayer © 1987 GIA Publications, Inc.
Music: David Haas (b. 1957) © 1987, GIA Publications, Inc.
You must contact GIA Publications, Inc. to reproduce this selection.

St Patricks Celtic

CHAPTER 5

Nature

When I am walking in the woods, or on the beach, in hillside fields or green glens I always look up to the sky. That's where I find my beloved clouds and rainbows, birds, treetops dancing and amazing color.

Then, like a captain surveying the horizon, I bring my eyes down and look all around me, 360 degrees, turning to survey the scenes, to hear the sounds, to see the birds, the butterflies, the squirrels, the flowering shrubs.

Finally, I look down, as I do mostly to make sure I'm walking on good ground, or flat sand. I kick away twigs or Spanish moss that have drifted down in their own journeys. I see pebbles and seashells, tree roots and small plants. What an amazing carpet of colors and shapes.

I'm very happy when I am near water. If it is the ocean, I listen to the heartbeat of the waves. If it is a lake I'm standing by, I watch the wind rippling across and I see birds skittering as they land on the surface.

For many years I lived on one of the Finger Lakes in upstate New York. Cayuga Lake is forty miles long, five miles at its widest and in some areas over five-hundred feet deep.

It is a glacial lake. As a child I swam every day in the summer, not realizing that its coldness was part of history. I sailed on it many years and learned to read the water, the winds and the currents like a map.

I collected sea glass and lucky stones, pottery shards from centuries of farmland runoff.

That lakeshore was as comfortable to me as my living room, because it *was* my living room.

Pebbles glistening, ducks with their little ones swim-skittering along the shore.

Now I live near the Gulf of Mexico and seashells and broken stones, sharks' teeth, beach flowers, tens of kinds of shore birds ranging from tiny plovers to huge seagulls and pelicans are my constant companions.

Looking down I see little bubbles in the sand where little crabs are busy. Looking straight out to the horizon I see where the sky meets the water, turning around I see the dunes and palmetto scrubs and looking up I see (yes, I do), a rainbow.

Nature for me is myself in the real world. Sometimes I feel it is the only place where I will be at peace and find truth.

I feel alive, my senses are watching, listening, seeing, hearing and smelling the world. My heart responds, as a child would, to a surprise sight, a special flower or creature, a sweet bunny rabbit or a large sandhill crane walking near me. Wow! I don't have to talk about it. I don't have to explain it. I don't have to do anything except be in the present moment with a world that is as ancient as the earth and as new and fresh as a morning breeze on my face.

I like quiet nature because it calms me. Thunderstorms and lightning and high winds make me anxious because they are so dramatic and carry with them such force that things can get harmed. But I know that the true soul of Nature in any form carries death as well as life. That is its great mystery.

I'm writing of Nature as it is in the physical world. I'm not smart enough, despite an entire career in nursing and health education, to talk about the nature of the human body. I have little true understanding of animals and vegetation or minerals and all I can do is respect and wonder at all Life as I think I know it is.

I do know that we are totally connected as humans, to the earth's bounty and the earth's beauty. I do know we have to honor and nurture our interdependencies with the Natural world if we are to stay alive as a species.

I know it is hard enough as a human being to be patient and caring, attentive, still, vigilant and respectful to other humans.

I know it's even harder to learn and listen to the language of the Natural world, which is not English-speaking.

Birds, trees, animals, insects, the wind, the water, all speak about their needs, their lives, their realities. Listening means I have to learn Nature as a second language.

Another human requirement for understanding and embracing our Natural world is that we must understand the collectiveness of our lives. No tree bears fruit on its own schedule. No farmer reaps his crop without having first planted seeds in the soil. No honeybee will survive if it can't find the sweet nectar of a blossom.

Survival means all of us, all of it, always.

Nature stuns me sometimes. I have read about the ancient peoples of the world and how they took remedies for survival from their Natural world. Today there is a wealth of information on natural remedies, spices and concoctions, foods and beverages made from plants and animals. Why wouldn't I be humbled to think that one herb could cure me and another could

kill me? It's all so much larger than I can imagine, this world of Nature.

For me, there is spiritual refuge in quiet natural spaces. I feel God when I stop and watch the clouds.

I feel like I'm in a sacred grove when I am in the woods. For me, trees are links between heaven and earth.

When I see a full moon in a clear night sky with Venus shining in a focus of white above it, I feel the presence of the force, the spirit, the mystery of life. I call it God. I call it Love. I see life renewed when I see a spring lilac and I see life at peaceful end when I see a rose petal fall to the ground.

Old life always has new life in it and new life always has old life in it and that is what nature shows me.

When I'm swimming in a lake or the ocean, or an outdoor pool and I look up to the sky doing my backstroke, I see angels in the clouds, their white feathery wings slowly moving. On the same day I walk a quiet autumn beach and see a magnificent rainbow at the eastern horizon as the sun is setting in the west.

In autumn, in the northeast, one of the sky's gifts to me would be the sight of the Canadian geese flying high in formation heading south, the blue sky meeting their black wings their squawking as they tell each other "Stay close, keep up!" Connected by air and spirit they leave the cold climates.

I now live in the place they fly to, the Florida winters. And I know they will fly back when the time is right. Their internal compass is amazing and they know without being told when they can fly and where they have to be to have their babies. Home. Home.

Home is where spirit and mystery, where Love and Life are in Nature.

Pablo Neruda, the Chilean poet wrote:

"Let us look for secret things somewhere in the world in the blue short of silence or where the storm has passed."

"I have wandered the earth in search of Life. Bird by bird I have come to know the world."

CHAPTER 6

The Italian Family

I grew up in an Italian family. After the Second World War, my father, a surgeon, returned to America from his duties in Britain, and told my mother he wanted to leave New York City and go upstate to live.

That must have been a shock for my mom. She had been taking care of her widowed mother, her first-born daughter and her three siblings in their Bronx home while her husband was gone. She was a city girl.

My father's parents and siblings were in Brooklyn and they too were surprised that their Carmine would leave them all for the farms of upstate New York! What was he thinking?

As I look back on my father's decision all these decades ago, I think I understand the structure of his decision. I certainly do not have a clue as to what was in his heart.

I believe my father returned to America, after a devastating absence from his wife and daughter, his parents, siblings and friends, with a traumatic memory of war, not a serene memory of the British countryside where his hospital was located. I believe he needed in his soul, the green hills, lakes and waterfalls, farms and sweet towns of upstate New York. The quiet healed him.

Ithaca, New York, a small town, a small county in the Finger Lakes region of mid-upstate New York—far enough away from city noise, traffic and crowds, but still only a four- or five-hour drive back to New York City.

With Cornell University and Ithaca College, this city was a sweet historic college town—perfect for a young, successful, brilliant surgeon to locate, set up his practice, and raise his family.

Except … in the late 1940s, upstate New York didn't have any Italian doctors! In fact, in Ithaca (not Syracuse or Rochester, Buffalo or Utica where more Italians had settled), the only Italian families lived in a sweet small section of the town and plied their trades as grocers, restaurant owners, craftsmen—men who built beautiful buildings and worked with their hands.

My father and one other doctor were the only Italian doctors in the entire county. Their colleagues were all non-Italians. I suppose he should have been used to his singular lack of fellow countrymen. In Columbia University and then Columbia Medical School, he was one of two graduating Italians in 1938.

We arrived in Ithaca, my father and mother, sister and me as an infant, to begin our new life.

No child at any age knows his parents' life, their relationship to one another or others. They were, for me, Mom and Dad! What I do know is that I had an amazing childhood and was loved, nurtured, encouraged, praised, guided and accepted by two remarkable people.

My mother was a strong, generous, capable, funny, acerbic, energetic and very smart woman. She had managed her father's construction company in the Bronx, and travelled to Europe, was an equestrian, and raised her three siblings because her mother was a non-English speaking widow. My mother's college career ended when her father died, but she continued to learn, growing into a beautiful wealthy young woman.

On the day she met her husband-to-be, my father, they were both attending a tea dance, at Columbia Medical School. My mother had accompanied her younger brother who was now a fourth-year medical student.

"Hello," my handsome brown-eyed, black curly-haired, soft-spoken father said to my mother. "My name is Carmine Russo, and I'm pleased to meet you."

"Thank you," said my mother. "My name is Rose Anna Russo."

Later in life we heard this first encounter told a hundred times! My father was surprised and taken aback when my mom told him her name. He thought she was flirting with him, and that she was insinuating rather boldly that she was going to become his wife. (Little did he know.)

"Oh," Carmine answered, "that is very amusing. We hardly know each other."

Roseanna's big brown eyes widened, her sharp mind putting his words into a context she had not expected. She smiled, a radiant smile.

"I am really Rose Ann Russo. Maybe you know my brother, John Russo? He's over there near the tables?"

"Oh, yes! I do know John!" They both laughed, they danced together, drank tea, and fell in love that day.

Now, a number of years later they live in a beautiful town in upstate New York. My father was a founder of the local hospital and began his practice in a two-hundred-year-old Greek mansion in downtown Ithaca.

As a young child, I grew up in the apartment above his office, across the street from the Greek Orthodox Church and a few blocks away from the best Italian restaurant for miles around.

Across from the Greek Church and my father's office was the Church of the Immaculate Conception. I was raised Catholic, but neither of my parents attended church regularly. Our aunt, my mother's sister, had moved to Ithaca with her doctor husband, so they used to take us.

My life from the moment I began to record and retain memory was totally Italian. During the first years I was fed the best homemade food in the world. We were dressed beautifully and strictly taught manners, respect and proper behaviors. Music was always playing on our radio.

My younger brother came along when I was six years old. My parents built a home in a very coveted neighborhood, high up on the hills near Cornell, overlooking the lake.

It was there that being a young Italian girl and then a rebellious teen, I lived for real as a spiritual adventurer. There is where my memories truly begin.

Inside that beautiful home were the possessions that define me to this day: my grandmother's tables and her china, my other grandmother's jewelry and art work, and my mother's kitchen, the sacred place of any Italian's home.

I have years of memories of family gatherings, visits from cousins, aunts and uncles from the city we had left, and our trips down to see them, often shopping in Manhattan's stores where my mom had shopped years ago.

My mother didn't work outside her home. Her kitchen office desk was where she managed the family's finances. It was close to the kitchen counters where she'd prepare her meals, listen to music, and tend the flowers on her kitchen ledges.

She loved nature and as a young girl to this very day, I am more comfortable in the woods, near a lake, on a hilltop, or in a garden, on a ski slope or skating on a frozen pond than I am around people. She taught me all this.

My father was an artist and a craftsman in his spare hours. He would often come home from a long day in the operating room and go to his "studio" and paint.

Both of my Italian parents were well-read, loved to hear and tell stories, and loved their family—valued their time at home and cared for their children with grace, bravery, humor, sincerity and a love that I thank God for every day.

Of course, all cultures honor their own. My life as an Italian in an upstate New York Eden had one flaw. Other cultures did not honor or accept us at the level of success my parents stood proudly. As a result, my mother stayed a loner among the townspeople while my father, through his reputation, skill, sweetness and accessibility became a much honored man. However, he, too, kept to himself.

I felt always out of place at school. As a teenager and for a long time, I felt I was different from most of my acquaintances.

I have always related more to others who aren't part of the WASP culture. There I said it. I recognize the kind of pride that lives inside of any immigrant culture, despite their outward American accomplishments.

I suppose if some of our non-Italian neighbors knew that my father's grandfather owned one of the largest pasta factories and companies in Italy, they may have given him a kinder hello.

If they knew my mother's father was a well-known and respected builder of many buildings in the Bronx, she would have been more accepted, as well.

What really matters is that we knew who we were, we all knew how we got to America, how our families worked, achieved and sacrificed for their families. We had a pride inside of our hearts and minds that just kept humming along.

As I learned piano, art, and ultimately my nursing, teaching and professional talents blossomed. I have always thought of myself as an Italian first—the rest can follow if it wants to!

That is why when I was in my mid-forties, already established and married, I embarked on a great journey to become an Italian citizen.

It took me five years. I had to apply in person to the Italian Consulate in New York City with original documents—birth certificate, parents' citizenships, marriages of grandparents on Italian letterheads obtained in the small communes, or villages where they lived.

Because this was prior to the terrorist attacks on the World Trade Center, the Italian government allowed someone who was born of an Italian currently living, to declare dual citizenship.

It took me many trips to New York City to obtain originals of my parents' documents and of my own, and to have all documents signed by Italian and American government officials.

Finally, in the mail, not long after I had returned from Ellis Island in the New York Harbor and saw with my own eyes the names of my ancestors as they arrived here, I received a letter. I have this letter framed in my cache of Italian papers. It was one of the proudest days of my life to become a dual-citizen in America and Italy! Italy and America!

The letter was accompanied by a sweet post-it from an Italian woman named Nancy, who was a registrar for the consulate. She wished to say, "Congratulations."

The letter, in Italian (which I read having taught myself the language and in many, many travels to Italy, have managed to learn the basics) said that I had satisfied a successful registration process, having proved my authentic heritage through proper documents and was now officially a citizen of the country of Italy!

Years later, now living in Florida, I have been separated by time and place from my heritage but I am still a typical Italian woman: passionate, smart, sassy, accomplished, bossy, critical, generous, an amazing cook, a pianist, a writer, a dreamer, a traveler, a basically warm embracing soul, a spiritual if not necessarily traditional woman, a devoted wife, an opinionated, sweet woman of a European country like no other in this world. Above all, I am proud to have been raised in a family, a culture, a special time in America where Italian values of family, love, bonding, respect, arts, culture, education, good food, loyalty and humility are essential attributes. Grazie molto, Dio.

My parents both came from families near Naples, Italy. When Garibaldi "united" Italy, he really didn't. I say that because the northern cities of Italy never truly accepted the cities and peoples of southern Italy after the 19th Century.

Naples had had a king of its own. Cities like Bari and Sicily in the boot of Italy are populated by a different mentality than you see in Milan, Florence, or Rome. Be that as it may, the Neapolitans are known for their sassy defiances, their sometimes crude and blustery but always funny takes on all things—life, food sex, marriage. You name it, the Neapolitans already have a phrase, a song, an insult or a hand or facial gesture for it.

I'm going to give you some of the phrases I grew up with when we were fighting, or joking or opining or just letting off steam.

Mind you, these phrases and sayings are just as much a part of Italy's fabric as is the opera, the Vatican, Capri, Florence or any poet, opera, Ferrari, or pasta dish. Enjoy and laugh, also Grazie and Ciao! And, remember, when Italians love you, they bring a whole family into your heart!

Some Italian Sayings and Quotes

- Mangia poco, bene, e spesso.
  Eat little, well, and often

- A tavola, sis ta sempre in allegria.
  At the table, one is always happy.

- Meglio pasta e fagioli a casia propria che pizza dolce a casa degli altri.
  Better pasta and beans in your own home than cake at the home of others.

- Carne e pesce ti fanno vivere a lungo.
  Meat and fish make you live a long time.

- "Save and you have" Rosie Russo

- "Your freedom ends at the tip of my nose." Carmine Russo

- Casa mia, casa mia, per piccina che tu sia, tu mi sembri una badia.
  My house, my house, as small as you are, you resemble an abbey.

Neopolitan Vocabulary (Not for the faint-hearted)

Che brute face! What an ugly face!	Non schiavettza! I'm not a slave!	Ella Princepessa! She's the Princess!
Strom balata! Strange!	Chiacchiera! Yakkety yak!	Ma chi e? Who's that!
Lo scemo! The fool!	Stropiata! Clumsy!	Furbo! Cunning!
Che cose cossi! What do you want?	Pazza! Crazy!	Va via! Go … away!
Sciatto! Slovenly!	Basta! Enough!	Andiamo! Let's go
Scorpo! Dirty!	Vattene Go away!	Io commincia! Now, it starts!
Chio' ceiola mi aspetta! I'm waiting for the Snail	Buffone! Clown!	Sta Zitto! Be … quiet!
Sta corta! Be Careful!	Minaccia Threat!	Mon oggio, Dio! God, what a day!
Mia off ana I'm breathless	Impazzire To go crazy	
Que voglie? You want what?	Che schifo! How disgusting!	

CHAPTER 7

The Languages of Our World

*H*ave you looked up the definition of the word, *language*? Webster's Dictionary states that among other explanations, language is "the expressions and communication of emotions or ideas between human beings by means of speech, either written or spoken."

As I looked further down the six other entries I was checking to see if they mentioned other species, other creatures or natural events where sounds mean something.

What about bird song or thunder? What about a violin concerto or a child's laughter? What about the sweet sound of a kiss?

What about two humans embracing? What about kittens snuggling against their mother's belly? Are those languages?

What about the sound of gunfire on a hot summer night or the sounds of a fist-fight or a siren?

I found an entry (#4) that gave me a definition of the word 'language' that satisfied me. It defined it as, "the transmissions of emotions or ideas between any living creatures by any means."

Oh, I thought, that is good. That definition covered the languages of the natural world. Then I looked for an entry that would cover symbolic sounds, like music, songs, chants, and non-verbal expressions. I found (#2) a simple statement that sufficed.

The vocal sounds or their written symbol used in such expression and communication.

That made me very happy, because I believe that language means a great deal more than spoken words, translated sentences from one country to another.

The key words to me are communication, expression, emotions, ideas, symbolic gestures and certain sounds.

The Latin word "lingua," which means 'tongue,' is the core of the word "language," but there is so much more to think about.

The Languages of Our World

Like any child growing up I lived in the culture of my family, its origins, its definitions, its habits and activities. As an Italian-American child whose parents were raised by Italians, I learned at a very early age that gestures, body motions, eye and visual motions, were the way we communicated. Music, always being played either on the piano or stereo was as much a part of my life as eating.

When I was entering high school, I took Spanish, French, German and Latin. My father advised me to learn Latin because it was the root of our tree of romance languages.

When my parents didn't want us children to know what they were saying, they spoke only Italian.

Some cultures have very animated ways of communicating and behaving. Others are more quiet and still. Nature was my second world. When I was not in the house or at school or inside somewhere, I was outside. I grew up in northern New York and my world was the four seasons. My sounds were the running water trickling in our backyard stream, and the constant birdsong of robins, sparrows, hawks. In my backyard I heard the pine trees constantly swishing and sighing. I listened acutely to raindrops and thunder and I could see and hear storms coming over the hills, across our lake, towards my bedroom window, where I would stand, watching.

I was attuned to sounds, to people's emotional and facial gestures, and to the words spoken all around me in school, in church, at friends' houses. I always sought connection to the world I lived in and now I see I was truly multilingual.

Stop for a moment and ask yourself what language you speak? Which, if you speak several, do you like the best? Are you a dancer, or a pianist, or are you someone listening to podcasts or audio books or the hundreds of sound media avenues for communicating?

Ask yourself if there are sounds in the sky. Have you ever heard a dolphin's song as it leaps out of the water? Do you live in a city where sounds communicate every urban event?

Do you hug people? Does your cat or dog look at you with eyes that speak volumes?

Do you Sudoku or enjoy math puzzles? Do you play a musical instrument? Do you know sign language or anyone who needs to use it?

Do you learn a few words to get by if you are travelling in another country? What language do you speak?

In our human world sounds matter so much. Hearing a language is different from reading a language. The words out of our mouths have emotion inflection, context, levels of meaning, signals of sound to the receiver. Words on paper are without sounds or motion, even as they conjure up an image or a feeling.

Some cultures, not European or Latin-based, but Native American, Eastern, African, and Asian, speak words that don't necessarily separate gender or tense. Inanimate objects, verbs, nouns, pronouns, all can take on a different meaning, a wider, more spiritual, universal tone.

In some cultures, stones, fire, and even stars speak. Humans speak with their hearts and the wisdom of their ancestors. Not all sounds have to be words.

Vision is also a language. And we don't just communicate with eyesight, but also with eye-signals. One look from an angry mom can stop a child in its tracks—one sweet loving gaze into your loved ones eyes speaks the language of your body, spirit, mind and heart.

Dream images and visual stories are language—movies, television, iPhones, TikTok, and YouTube are all languages of images.

I can stand for hours and look at a hawk or eagle flying with high clouds behind it. I can sit on a garden and watch bees hop from blossom to blossom, or see a monarch butterfly swoop and flutter by me. I feel connected, "communing" with the world in which I live.

(Communication's root word is communes, Latin for share/common.)

Our five senses (touch, taste, hearing, speech, vision) were not accidental items passed through the eons of human existence. These senses guaranteed our survival and they still do, despite modern man's arrogance.

I call it arrogance because I've seen in my own lifetime—a global phenomenon of disrespect for cultures not our own and an isolating attitude that "my world is better than your world."

Instead of embracing other cultures and values different from or even opposite of ours, we shut down an important portal to understanding the wisdoms and teachings of others, which would connect us, comfort us, and ensure our survival.

It is too easy to hurt someone virtually now, to slander or abuse someone by a text message. It doesn't require the five senses to send an email or text. But it does require the five senses to survive.

All language, verbal, tactile, silent or visual requires us to be together as a species, to stay connected to one another.

If we lose our abilities to use our language skills, whatever form they take, we will lose our souls, the animated passions we use in writing, speaking, playing music, dancing, or touching one another.

CHAPTER 8

Nanny's Quotes

- Assess – Affirm – Accept
- You can't look back and regret your life—you can only regret not celebrating it.
- Let me make today the most fully alive day I have ever known.
- Some never understand the value of people—they are obsessed with the importance of things and money.
- Don't judge others: judge yourself.
- Is there any chance of happiness without Faith?
- A lot of things can be done without grace, but they won't make you happy.
- Talk to people in the language they understand. Don't try to be clever or evasive. Talk straight in the words you both know and the charity between you will do the rest.
- Some people hold on to memories, others hold on to hope.
- She is as useless as a dull pin.
- You can lose a pin inside a pincushion if you push it too hard!
- Have you ever looked at a painting of yours or a book you wrote, or something you handmade and seen it as the work of a stranger? Where did that come from? I did that?
- When profit is a motive, kindness suffers.
- Politics serve self-interests, not the greater good.
- The very wealthy need to play the politics game so they can protect and enhance their accumulated wealth.
- The wealthy prosper from avoiding taxes and embracing prestige. They play a serious game of jumping into loop holes.
- The only thing I have in my war chest is love.
- If you stand in the middle, turn around and see 360 degrees. You won't be able to look backwards and forwards at the same time.
- Trust is not Faith. Faith is not Love.
- Keep looking for your truth North.
- Surrender and Breathe!
- We live our lives alone in the company of others.
- There is always a gift at the other side of surrender.
- Death is not scary. Life is.
- Health is wealth is Freedom. Don't waste it!
- Problems have solutions. Mysteries don't.
- Hope is born from misery.
- Doing acts of kindness and charity keeps your spirit happy.

- A good teacher asks very good questions. The word, "educator" comes from Latin "educe," which means "to bring things out of you."
- A good teacher can bring great thoughts out of students.
- A good student listens to truly learn.
- What and who teaches us?
  - Real life
  - Parents
  - Educators
- All learning always goes back to humility, love, patience and acceptance.
- You cannot ask what you do not know needs asking.
- Justice and Fairness flourish in the open.
- EAT, PRAY, LOVE — SIT, TEXT, GET STUPID.
- Can anyone trace the upper class British accent?
- This is a world of replaceable parts.
- You have to work really hard not to waste Grace every day.
- Life is a mist that vanishes.
- Tomorrow is unknown.
- Be patient and endure. Pray. Prayer is powerful.
- Tame your tongue. You can't be holy with a nasty tongue.
- Young people are LIVING this life.
- Old people are LEAVING this life.
- A great many old people wait for yesterday to return and they hope for tomorrow, but what do they do today?
- A lot of old people don't realize or accept how irrelevant they now are.

Nanny wish list as she ages:
  - Always stay in tune with my heart-song
  - Always teach myself something new.
  - Use my mind well
  - Hold my soul in my hands and do God's work
  - Watch things
  - Know life
  - Find joy in the smallest details.
  - Understand people in my life
  - Stay close to my loved ones always, if not physically then verbally.
  - Read, read, read!
  - Write!
  - Cook better Italian recipes!
  - Do jigsaw and crossword puzzles!
  - Keep playing the piano.

- The hardest thing I have to do in my life is to stay focused and sit still, to listen to what I must be and do, and to NOT be afraid to look inward. I must have courage to do these things.
- Simple living, which I strive for daily, is really hard. I can't be ignorant, but must stay humble and grateful and graceful.
- Pray ... ask ... wait ... pray ... ask ... wait ... pray ... ask ... wait ...
- The life I seek requires tremendous courage, stamina and wisdom.
- My life, and yours, is a tapestry. In any crisis we see two things:
  - A shredding of the woven truths of our lives
  - A need to find new threads, new colors and images for our tapestries going forward.
- Every day NOT spent loving and living in the service of God is a waste of time and life.
- Vanity is insanity.
- Smiling makes you beautiful.
- Some people desire security and seek attachments to others for comfort and confirmation. Sometimes they find an angel mate; other times they find a detached or broken mate.
- Seek peace inside yourself and you will see it in others.
- Be careful in your embraces and rejections of the people around you.
- Some people embrace Nature and reject Society.
- Some people are givers. Some people are takers.
- A good simple life is a kind peaceful faith, with routines and tasks blessed by grace, deep in peace and wide in charity.
- The more you try to avoid suffering, the more you suffer. Small things begin to scare you.
- We all have to suffer sometimes. You cannot avoid it.
- Depression is anger turned inward. A quiet sadness replaces the angry outbursts.
- Everyone has to find their own way home.
- Everyone needs Hope.
- Some people face defeat and are rescued. Others face defeat and are lost.
- Sometimes you have to be emptied to be filled again.
- Pay attention to the silence, not the noise.
- It is vast and eternal and into it you must fly.
- Old life always has new life in it. New life always has old life in it.
- Stubbornness and ignorance are a really bad combination!
- Everyone has got something to say. Not everyone thinks before they say it.
- Not everyone listens. They don't know how to control their egos.
- Stupidity and naivety are a perfect combination for extinction.
- Greed, cowardice and ingratitude can't exist between friends.
- Everyone becomes a predator when food is scarce.
- If you touch something, study it and try to understand it, try to see what it truly is.
- Criminals are cunning and victims are naïve.
- Is Fate coincidence? Is coincidence Fate?

- Sometimes we stumble into chance and everything changes.
- Trust your own instincts.
- Be careful who and what you believe.
- Did you ever think that you can disguise yourself or lie to others without consequences? You can't run away from your true nature.
- Forgiveness always restores whatever it touches, and greed always destroys whatever it touches.
- Nanny's theory of evolution:
  - Humans are derived from primates.
  - Primates are the only species with true opposing digits (hands).
  - Opposing digits are required to hold an iPhone, text, email, scroll, type.

Do you wonder why?

- Some people are cautious in the ways of an old soul.
- Once labeled, always defined.
- It is not how you die but how you live that counts and it is not how you lie but how you die that counts.
- Medieval knights wore heavy metal armor often weighing hundreds of pounds as they faced enemies in battle. The armor modern man wears isn't metal. Our armor these days is aggression, hostility, bullying, and impenetrable denials of truth. Our modern armor protects the weak and scared people who perceive danger all around them.
  - ✦ But … bravery, sweet calm acceptance, and outward seeking connections with others is the true armor.
  - ✦ Stand and face the world from within yourself—you don't need armor.
- What is inside of you is more precious than what is outside of you.
- Everything you need is already inside of you. Everything you *don't* need is as well. It's your choice, so act wisely.
- You are not the passenger of your body, but the driver.
- Discipline yourself to do simple things perfectly. Strive for that.
- When you walk, always look up as well as down.
- A Life = years = months = weeks = days = hours = minutes = seconds. Live it well.
- Learn to know and accept the softening that aging brings to your life.
- Words may not be as strong as silence.
- Always look for the hidden inside of things.
- Whatever you think you know about something is probably not the whole picture.
- If you miss a goal, reset it and aim again. Don't give up!
- Anyone can make a lie seem like a truth. People believe what they want to believe, not what is necessarily true.
- What is Truth? Think long and hard before you answer.
- Some people are doers. Some people are talkers. Some people are sitters. Some people are walkers.
- You don't ask a fireman to sit and fold napkins!

CHAPTER 9

Wisdom

What is wisdom? Is it the same thing as intelligence? Is wisdom knowledge? Is it science? Is it experience? Does wisdom require faith and acceptance? Can the curious be already wise? Is wisdom a "human-only" ability? Does wisdom require language? Are insight and intuition required for wisdom? Is common sense necessary for wisdom? Can the very young be wise or does wisdom require age and experience? Is wisdom more important than salvation? Does wisdom teach Peace and Acceptance to mankind?

Is wisdom divine?

Why do I care about wisdom to ask so many questions? I have always asked more than answered in my life and I have learned, observed, and read so many different subjects that I know only this; wisdom is a mystery.

If we read the ancient philosophers, or study science, learn theology, or follow a guru, we arrive at the same place. Knowing something can take many forms. Learning has been part of human existence since the beginning of our world.

Ancient cultures accepted wise words from elders, and learned to follow practices that kept their world intact. Before the written words were read, the rituals of faith, agriculture, social custom, and non-verbal communications connected man to one another and to the physical world he inhabited.

The world was here long before we were. We just didn't know enough about it, so we had to learn the rules and teach what we know to others so we can all survive.

Is it a pattern in all life, in all worlds, that truth and mystery are always present, while other subjects are apparent and on the surface or even hidden, requiring keys to open secret chambers? Is wisdom accessible to anyone seeking it?

Tradition has given us spokesmen for wisdom. You may be saying now, "She still hasn't defined "wisdom" yet." Actually, I may not be able to do that. Seers, prophets, scientists, philosophers, and healers have all spoken, sung, danced, preached, written, painted, and orated truths of life as they know them to be.

In civilization you need to have a language that others living with you, working and existing beside you, can understand. I think it is safe to say that traditional wisdom and cultural knowledge are taught through common action.

Listening, asking, looking at non-verbal clues, speaking, touching, and singing—this is how we communicate. Wisdom needs a form of communication, so that what is being taught and shared can continue beyond the moment.

If wisdom teaches truth, it also teaches how to ask questions to find truth. So to learn something, we must first observe, listen, converse, and ask why? How? When? Where? We must listen more than anything, if we want to accept wise words or teachings that are not our own. We can't live long enough to become as wise as centuries of teachings gift us in one reading.

In my own life, I have come to know wisdom in different ways. As a young independent woman, I learned by error that some things I did, said, or believed were just plain stupid.

I thought I respected knowledge. I was, after all, college educated, professionally certified, competent

in the arts, an avid reader, and a spiritual adventurer. I believed I knew how things worked in the universe.

Well, wisdom watched patiently over the years as I began to understand certain things. Wisdom healed my anger when nothing else could. Wisdom showed me that the stranger my opinions were, the larger my ignorance was.

Wisdom gently taught me to take all words seriously and to respect the words of others.

Wisdom showed me that the intelligence she required didn't come from books and that my world views, my beliefs and biases can place me either inside or outside of other's worlds or lives. She taught me that wisdom is a gift, often a lucky opportunity to experience knowledge, sometimes a sheer coincidence.

So now, still ignorant but humbled, still learning, but a bit wiser, I have come to believe (and act on those beliefs) that Faith, Humility, Grace, and Love is what wisdom is.

My life's lessons didn't end here—they begin here. I know that science, truth, philosophy, and all forms of learning and knowledge are essential to knowing some answers to a few questions.

I know that facts matter. I know that precision and understanding how things work matters. I know that science isn't truth and knowledge isn't wisdom. I know that if I "assess, affirm and accept" what is all around me, I will obtain some little piece of wisdom and that with the acceptance of that little gift, I will find peace.

The best part for myself in my own quest for the How's and Why's and When's and Where's and Who's of life around me, before me and after me is this—that once I have acquired a piece of wisdom I have it forever!

Wisdom never goes away once you have some. It is for me a Divine presence that watches me stumble, crawl, dance, walk, and throw my arms up to the sky in happiness.

I think once you have wisdom visit you, you always have that gift inside of you.

I think it is a good thing to pass what you know to others, so they too can learn and accept, and hopefully hold some of wisdom's hand someday.

You will read more quotes, stories, fables, parables in your own lives, so you don't need too many from my own, but what follows now are some wise sayings I have collected over the years.

I hope you recognize a happy and real connection to your heart, mind and soul when you read them. Wisdom smiles on us all.

- "Knowledge is not the same as understanding."
- "Through wisdom comes the perfection of love and power and knowledge."

Tau Malachi (1962 -) St. Mary Magdalene,
Bishop of Sophia Fellowship, writer

- "Life passes on in proximity to the sacred. It is this proximity that endows existence with ultimate significance."
- "The limitations of human understanding do not permit the prophet to see the fullness of the divine light. If not visible the prophet knows God is accessible."
- "Ritual makes us receptive to theology."

20th Century. A.G. Heschel
Rabbi/Theologian (1907 -)

- "I must study politics and war that my sons may have liberty to study mathematics and philosophy."

President John Adams
(1735 – 1826)

- "Problems have solutions; mysteries do not."

Religious Scholar Huston Smith
(1919 – 2016)

- "Fear precedes caution. Caution precedes bravery. Bravery precedes discovery. Discovery produces relief. Relief produces wisdom."

Unknown

- "You have to live spherically in many directions."

Italian film maker
Federico Fellini (1920 – 1993)

- "The world is a book. Those who do not travel read only one page."

Unknown

- "Our universe came into being as a miniscule speck of brilliant light. It was infinitely hot. Inside the fireball was contained the whole of space. And with the creation of space came the birth of time."

Sir Martin Rees (1945 -)
The British astronomer Royal, astrophysicist

- "Nothing has changed the nature of man so much as the loss of silence."

Swiss philosopher Max Picard (1888 – 1965)

- "Patience, patience, patience is what the sea teaches, Patience and Faith."

American author and aviator
Anne Morrow Lindbergh (1906 – 2001)
Gift from the Sea

- "The human heart remains, like a bulwark against nihilism. Heeding the heart, the desire to return home (its destiny) is the beginning of recovery. It seems like nothing, but it is what we need for recognizing the truth, if by chance truth comes our way."

Fr. Julián Carrón (1950 -)
Spanish priest & professor of theology

- "We have to unlearn hurrying. Plunging into something will get you into a deep hole."

Dr. Robin Wall Kimmer (1953 -)
Scientist, professor – member of Potawani
Indian Nation

- "The only permanence in this world of relative values is the permanence of memory."

Greek Historian Herodotus – (484 – 430 B.C.)
The Histories

The following five quotes are from Jean-Luc Picard 24th century starship captain, explorer, diplomat—fictional, but amazing character.

✦ "Our time in this universe is finite. That is one of the truths that all humans must learn"

Star Trek: The Next Generation
Season 3; Episode 5

✦ "There is no greater challenge than the study of philosophy."

Season 2; Episode 17

✦ "Seize the time! Live now! Make now always the most precious time. Now will never come again."

Season 5, Episode 25

✦ "Open your mind to the past. Art, history, philosophy. And all this may mean something"

Season 2, Episode 17

✦ "The search for knowledge is always our primary mission."

Season 1, Episode 7

- "As soon as man does not take his existence for granted but beholds it as something mysterious, thought begins."

- "Only when the human spirit grows powerful within us and guides us back to a civilization based on humanitarian ideal, will that spirit act for other peoples. All men are endowed with compassion and can develop a humanitarian spirit. There is inflammable matter within all men. Let there come a spark and it will burst into flames."

Dr. Albert Schweitzer (1875 – 1965)
Doctor, explorer, musician, minister, Nobel Prize winner

- "Peace between nations. Peace between neighbors. Peace between lovers in love of the God of Life, Peace between man and woman, parent and child, brother and sister of Christ above all peace."

Celtic Prayer from Iona
Hebrides, Scotland

- "Little else but weather ever happened in the treeless yellow hills to Black Elk's home, other than the sun and moon and stars going overhead. There was little for the old men to do but sit quietly and wait for yesterday."

John Neihardt (1881 – 1973)
Preface to 'Black Elk Speaks'
Poet, American historian

- "Sometimes dreams are wiser than waking"
- "Anywhere is the center of the world."
- "The thoughts of men should rise high as eagles do."

Black Elk, Oglala Lakota holy man & educator,
Cousin to Crazy Horse (1863 – 1950)

- "How should I live my life? Don't use your consciousness as a guide for living for it can never know why or how it sees things."
- "Apply your understanding of things to decide your best course and deliberately follow your decision."
- "Conscious knowledge, ethics, philosophy, human progress and purposeful activity all sit on elusive truths."

Chinese philosopher Zhuangszi
(369 BC - ? BC)

CHAPTER 10

Observations

Jorge, the Gardener, and Names in the Vineyard

Jorge is our gardener. He is the supervisor of ten Mexicans who take care of the seventeen acres of our condo property. I guess Jorge is in his mid-twenties. He speaks with a soft English accent and he always has a smile for me.

When I see his crew arrive, spilling out of the truck and getting their equipment ready, I come out and greet them, thanking them in Spanish (Italian style) and English with prayerful gestures for the good hard work they are doing for us. I bring them bottles of water as they labor in the hot sun.

One day, during the frantic and unruly days of high season when many of the tourists and renters are rude, clueless, careless and unfriendly, often littering the grass and sidewalks, I saw Jorge.

"I can't stand this!" I exclaimed to him. "These people drive me crazy!"

He looked at me. I saw the large golden crucifix he wore catch sunlight and it sparkled on his chest.

He smiled at me and said, "People do not know how to behave and act good to each other. So silly, so sad, for we are all we have is each other in this world and life is so short.

Earlier that year in the summer, two-thousand miles north, my husband and I were walking along a small road in the hills of the Finger Lakes. We were stopping at a vineyard on the west side of Seneca Lake and were walking down the hill from the winery buildings towards the water.

We passed hundreds of vines, full deep green and tall, laden with purple and green grapes.

Row upon row we walked by these plants, growing in orderly rows. Pegged and supported by wires, they covered acres of hillside. We stood at the end of one row and looked down at the deep blue water of this glacial northern lake. The sun warmed our faces and like the grapes, we bathed in its light.

At the end of each row of vines, a sturdy large post was anchored into the ground. On a large card on each of hundreds of these poles were written a few simple sentences: the name of the grape, the date it was planted and to our surprise, a first Christian Hispanic name, different for each post.

Carlos, Juan, Pedro, Estefan, Miguel, Roberto, and on and on the rows were named!! The names of the laboring Mexican crews who came every year were forever connected to the amazing vines, which offered the fruits of their labors!

In upstate New York the deep glacial lakes and their surrounding hillsides, creeks, and waterfalls have for millions of years strewn rock, stones, and wood into the waters.

As men began to inhabit this part of the earth, stones and rocks became important to their survival— sharp arrowheads for hunting, large boulders for barriers and fire-circles. And later on, the farmers and settlers poured broken china, glass and other objects into their hillside streambeds.

I grew up scouring the lakeshore for hidden treasures, beautiful glass, round river stones, and lucky stones (circles of long-gone iron leaving a perfect hole in the middle of each stone). I would look at a smooth stone or a piece of shale and see an animal, a bird or a flower shape. I'd bring my treasures home with me.

As the years went by, my collection of sea glass was astounding! I also had rare and beautiful pieces of porcelain.

I would paint many of the rocks and to this day, I have beautiful seagulls, whales, dogs, horses and flowers in my collection of painted stones. I was painting the image when the rock "spoke" to me and told me what to paint. Timeless messages. Also from those days, I have a collection of smooth round river stones. I paint words on them and place them on a large plate. "Love," "Mercy," "Patience," "Acceptance," "Faith," "Truth," "Spirit," "Humility," "Hope." Every time I pass by, the stones speak to me.

Sometimes I would find a sentence from Scripture or religious or spiritual works. I would paint a word on the stone on which I wanted the lesson to focus, then wrap it in linen with a verse of Scripture written on it and wrap it in a fine silk ribbon , then give it to someone.

I am simply a messenger. The rocks and stones come from eternity. I have a game I want to play with children. I call it, "Scripture Stones." All of Nature could play with us.

Rocks fit together. They are always touching. Large, small, rough, smooth. They write. Rock walls make me happy, for they create the ultimate pattern of connection and protection.

River stones nesting against each other or large stones create a patio or pathway that comforts me, because they relate continuously through time with their edges, curves and angles. They nest with their neighbors.

I have stone arrangements in my home. I can move them around and, as I caress and reposition them into new links and patterns, I feel an amazing calm, peace and quietness in my heart and soul.

The stones speak to one of ancient truths and pathways and I pray with them and smile.

Throughout my travels I have collected stones, glass and pottery shards. In my bowls at home are vestiges of cultures and places thousands of miles from here.

In Florida there are more seashells than sea glass and I collect them with the same reverence, gratitude and curiosity as of all others.

It amazes one how our earth keeps revealing such ancient truths so openly, literally under our footsteps.

Sarasota, Florida

Overheard at the luggage carousel in Sarasota Airport

A little girl was waiting with her daddy, holding his hand, as the luggage began to appear. She must have been five or six years old. "Daddy, what language do they speak here?"

Overheard at our optician's office

A grandmother was filling out a medical form for her young grandson who must have been six or seven years old. His little feet stuck straight out as he sat on the chair next to her.

"Jimmy, it asks here if you are having any trouble seeing," she said. "Are you?"

"Oh, no, Grandma!" he answered. "Only when my eyes are closed."

Thoughts on words: Words Matter

The word is "carry." What does it mean?

To bear, to sway, to drift, to ferry, to yield, to sail, to transport.

I know you cannot carry negativity if you seek truth and love nature.

Oscar Sherer Park, The Pine and the Bamboo

The Pine sways and softly swishes.

The bamboo click-clacks, rattling in the wind.

The sky is a deep, endless blue

The soft air smells of flowers.

I look up, my head bent all the way back

And see … an osprey, flying high and downwards.

He rests on a high branch in the pine.

Selby Gardens, Flower in a Pond

- Zentangle is making lines and figures, a free-form style of meditation. Mind, eyes, hands, pen, and paper are one.
- Patterns bubble up to the surface like petals of sea lilies in the pond.
- The lines, circles, shadows, and triangles transfer to the water like written ripples of oleander and palm leaves.
- Designs of motion and spirit, red roses among the lilies.

The Beach at Sunset, the Intracoastal Waterway, Siesta Key

She sits alone on the beach, facing the water, facing east.

The clouds are high, pink, pale blue, orange, absorbing in afterglow the western sunset.

The pelicans are returning to their mangrove beds to sleep for the night; the branches sway silently with the soft landings.

The water is rippling with fish and tidal currents.

The evening is quiet.

She begins to pray.

The Prisoners

In the south you still can see prison work crews.

Dressed in yellow or orange coveralls, and watched closely by men with guns.

Is their work honorable?

They look so young.

Is this all they have in this time on Earth?

The very Earth that they are raking?

New York State, A Walk in Central Park

- Small paths over old stone bridges, carved with curlicues and florets, their patterns casting shadows on the ground which is covered with acorns.
- Looking down at the path as I circle the reservoir, I see a bit of glitter. It is an earring. I thing some fast-running woman has lost it among the leaves that line the grass edge.
- I wonder if she misses it.

Ithaca, the Window Pane in Autumn

I lay on my bed on my back. Looking through the window I see the trees dancing in the wind, mostly green, but with some early yellows and reds, like the first gray hairs of a young woman's head.

Through the pane I see an opening in the pathway of light from me through the window to the trees and to the distant opening of the sky.

I close my eyes and see more. I see my childhood home, less than one mile away. I see myself as a child, laughing and playing in our backyard among the same kinds of trees as today I see swaying outside the window. As a child in my yard the trees were my friends, and they were my magical world.

I hear my laughter of sixty years ago and I feel my freedom as I played countless hours outside in all seasons.

I smile today with deep happiness. I am home again after a long absence. How ironic to be living now less than a mile from what will always be my true home.

The Sounds of Well-Being in the World

- Clanking silverware as you pass an open – someone is eating.
- Dogs barking
- The Sound of birds

My Apron

I love my apron. I am happy to put it on ,because it means I am going to cook for my husband.

I am going to touch food, form it, and create Love with simple action and gratitude

Things I think about with no answers. I don't want answers

1. Motion and rest
2. God in nature
3. The duality of all things
4. The soul's journey
5. Mind, body, spirit
6. Childlike wisdom
7. Peace is within
8. Male – female - male
9. Earth mother
10. Sky father
11. Water mother and father
12. Music, poetry and art are man's gift to the world
13. What triggers laughter? Surprise, embarrassment, inconsistencies, recognition, ambivalence, emotional release, insecurity, sincerity, puzzles answered

The Mirror

- I talk to my mirror a lot. I am best friends with my reflection, my oldest friend.
- I make serious faces. I make goofy faces.
- Sometimes I see pain. Other times I see anger.
- I tell the woman looking back at me to smile and I look pretty then.
- I see my mother in my face and expressions
- I comfort the "worried" woman, pray a little and say "this too shall pass"
- I count my blessings and I roll my eyes
- I give myself advice and I chide myself for being a jerk
- I can be whoever I want to be when I look in the mirror
- I always see a true friend, one I can laugh with!
- I understand this woman. She is me.
- The mirror shows my heart and soul.

CHAPTER 11

Words Inside, Words Outside

Have you ever thought about something and made a silent or spoken remark about it that you repeated at different times to others or yourself?

Have you silently cursed, laughed, wondered, or sarcastically approached something or reflected upon a reality with which you were dealing?

Do you have you people in your life with whom you automatically make one-liners or share funny quips when you see one another?

Have you ever repeated proverbs, sayings our parents and their parents used it to teach us or simple sentences or sometimes longer stories with endings that impart something, like a fable, a lesson, or a quotation? I have.

Here are some of them.

Chess

- Every chess-player knows one thing—you must outsmart your enemy to survive.
- He plays chess like a genius, but doesn't live his life like me.
- A chessboard has squares just like a crossword puzzle does. Chess is a motion-oriented problem-solving puzzle.
- Nancy's chess life-story;
  - She was taught to play as a young girl by her patient father.
  - Her brain fogs over every time, and she has tried often. She even reads books on how to play chess.
  - She is an impulsive player who can't sit still long enough to think more than two moves ahead.
  - Her husband, with whom she plays every day, is a quiet, logical thinker who studies the board for long periods to develop strategies for many moves ahead.
  - Nancy loses a lot because she is multitasking, sometimes doing a crossword puzzle while she waits for him to move.
  - She sees chess as a battle, a fight for life, a scary thing, sometimes asking "chexist" questions like:
    1. Why does the queen have to do all the work, while the king sits safely behind his guards in his castle, huh?
    2. I know the queen is the only female in the game, so why don't I ever see the many threats she has to fight off, even though she is the most powerful player?
  - Chess is an allegory for life. There's always a death at the end, sometimes many victories, sometimes the stalemate shows reconciliation, and sometimes great fortunes come from the mistakes of others.
  - Pawns, the little things in life, often make the big things (the king's safety) happen.

Crosswords

- Like chess, crossword puzzles use squares. Instead of pieces, words are the primary actors.
- When you enter the right word in place, you have met not only the puzzlemaker's challenge. You have challenged your own mind, your own experience, with language and words to supply the correct answer.
- Crossword puzzles use a different form of logic than chess. You must look at space, at the definition, at formation of another word waiting nearby that must go either up or down inside or beside your answer.
- Unlike chess, crossword puzzles have answer sheets. Need I say more?

Jigsaw Puzzles

- The satisfaction in placing the right piece of a jigsaw puzzle into the correct position has a right-brain–left-brain digit connection that neither chess nor crossword puzzles have. Chess pieces are picked up and moved all over the board. The pencil you hold to enter the answers to a crossword puzzle is only used to inscribe something the brain is telling you to write.
- But in putting a jigsaw piece in place, especially one you have worked for a long time to find, you first must look at it carefully for clues, usually with a magnifying glass. Then you have to view the total puzzle picture and look for connections, relationships and possibilities. This all takes time. So when your fingers hold the piece and snap it into its rightful place, there is a happy click in your brain too! I love that feeling!

Lessons from Puzzles and Chess

1. Knowing how something works doesn't teach you what something means.
2. Over time, and with experience and effort, you learn both.

One-Liners

- Wealth is freedom. Health is freedom. Don't waste them.
- It's easy to say things. It's impossible to "unsay" things. Once out, it's out ….
- Happiness is a personal choice and a personal responsibility.
- The patterns and connections of nature are reassuring.
- The wind is the breath of the earth, the waves hitting the shore is its pulse.
- Prayer on a spring morning walk:
- –Thank you for this place
- –For my life full of grace
- –For high flying birds in blue space
- –For the sun shining on my face
- Memories, tears and smiles are prayers.
- Touching and holding someone is a prayer.
- Swimming laps daily is a blessing, a baptism, a necessity, and a rebirth.
- The world would be a more peaceful and happier place, if everyone swam every day.
- Smiling makes you beautiful.

•Florida's new state motto: NO ACRE LEFT UNDEVELOPED

•If you want to truly communicate with another human being, you must know the language he speaks and use it back to him. People understand the language they speak: words of bullies, words of preachers, teachers, or saints, or words of soldiers. Learn this language and then speak back in the same tongue.

The Irony of Social Media and Cell Phones

- Social media is a Happiness Trap of perpetual irrelevance.
- Eat, pray, love? Sit, text, get stupid!
- The only times humans are quiet and still are when they are sleeping, or when they are sitting glued to their cell-phones.
- Here's the irony:
  + The internet with its many platforms can be creative, informative, lucrative, entertaining and educational.
  + At the same time, social media can be aggressive, violent, stupid, misinforming, malignant, and irrevocably damaging.

    Social media platforms, cell phones, laptops, and notebook screens when used with earbuds cover the sounds of the real world. Users are swept into often narcissistic worlds filled with loud, frequently angry words, blaring music and jarring sound effects.

    The sound of what is happening *inside* the brains of users is not the same as what is happening *outside* their bodies.

    Just look at the quiet, rapid-fire continuous tapping of fingertips on four-by-six-inch piece of plastic. The human animal is totally and silently absorbed as they check their phones every chance they can—never looking up, never saying a word to those nearby, whether sitting at a bus-stop, a restaurant booth or in a grocery-line—no human interaction with real-life people all around them. Just silent soft taps of fingers on lifeless keyboards.

> **Connection or Isolation?** No human voice is required, no face-to-face, eye-to-eye touching, or smiling. No visible clues or signals from living bodies in connecting to what is invisible to others—all quiet and extremely deadly, if not understood for what it *really* is.

♥

CHAPTER 12

Human Nature

- Human beings are very complicated. As a species we have survived for thousands of centuries. We have evolved from primitive beings. We have cultural, mental and physical traits that have guaranteed our existence. We have individual DNA and RNA, but our survival as humans depends upon our ability to connect with one another. We need society for survival.

- We have a responsibility to the survival of own species. We have to pull together, work together, believe in the "common good." We must think of others, take our responsibilities and possibilities seriously. We can't take our survival, individually or as a species, for granted. No one gets a free ride.

- What is human emotion? What are human traits? How do we learn to be human? What separates us from other species? What connects us to other species?

- Are there deep truths in our DNA?

- It is no coincidence that "opposites" and "connections" flow through our humanity. We must connect to others to communicate. We have to connect with the wind and stars, the sun and moon, water, rocks, trees, birds, animals, flowers, clouds and all of Nature to know our own humanity.

- Let's explore some "opposites" and decide which traits would encourage longevity, peace, gratitude, sweetness, humility, patience, intelligence and happiness and how the opposites of these traits endanger us as a species and the very earth we call HOME.

  - ✦ Peace – Actions we take, thoughts we think, or lessons we teach our children to live with harmony inside our hearts, family rooms, schoolyards, shops, and our places of work and worship.

  - ✦ War – To fight against others with whom we don't agree, to choose violence towards people and places we don't understand or see as a threat. To decide individually that we are right and others are wrong and must suffer, to isolate others in families and community to keep them vulnerable.

- Humility - To know what we don't know is so much more than what we think we know. To accept our vulnerability as humans and to rely upon our instincts to serve others. To recognize our responsibility to give more to others, to family, to mates, to friends, and to strangers than we would take from them. To know we cannot exist alone and to rely on the goodness of others, just as they rely on our caring of them. To know that loving is the most difficult human endeavor of our species. To crave silence, peace, and detachment and to elevate those around us through acts of kindness.

  [humility comes from Latin "humus"
  meaning ground, earth, down-to-earth]

- The opposite of humility has many forms: arrogance, pride, violence, contempt for others, selfishness, materialism, impatience, greed, deception, or anger.

- All of these, if left unchecked or unchallenged, will ruin the human species, because none of these traits are compatible with peace and preservation.

- Human beings need to think before they act. Our "intelligence" appears to be superior to other species, but as Native Americans, ancient philosophers, and wise men throughout the ages know:
- Humans are controlled by instincts, which are really significant, because they show us what we need to know, huge amounts of hidden data, facts and evidence.
- Instincts lead us to thinking. Logic comes after we know something. Instinct gives us the acceptance of something.
- Why do humans weep and mourn? How do they accept sorrow? How does our species honor life and accept death? How can both grief and joy bring tears? How do we accept the world around us? I believe it is called *grace*.
- We couldn't survive as a species without grace. I cannot define grace, however, I do know that love grace, humility, and gratitude are in our DNA as a species.
- I do know that as humans we KNOW LOVE WHEN WE FEEL IT.
- Grace gives us joy, innocence, belief in beauty, love of nature. It came with us, or to us, as we emerged from the ancient embryos of our species.
- No one can eliminate love, grace, or joy from the human race. It seems that man's heart, often grieving or afraid or full of loss, can have happiness, joy, and sweetness at the same time.
- The simple truth is that since he has written symbols on cave walls, the human species has recognized and honored a force much greater than his earthly beliefs.
- That force might be called God, or any of thousands of names. I call it "Truth," and I believe it preceded humanity. The human species knows that truth, love, grace and its behaviors are the secret to their survival.
- The more we as humans know ourselves, who we are, and what we do that is right and moral and true, the more we know about the depth of our universe, because we become connected to the mysteries. We know we won't solve them, but we will always contemplate them.
- We all know, without being told, when someone has given us a sweet, loving, safe space.
- We recognize love when it is shown to us.
- Children automatically laugh at funny things. They cannot explain and often don't even understand. They know they are little, instinctively. They know without being shown that they are in Love's presence. They feel neither pride nor shame or confusion. It is human nature.
- It is in our human nature to be playful and earnest, relaxed, healthy and vigorous. We often ignore these traits, replacing them with gravity, anxiety, laziness, lassitude. Thus, we become vulnerable and begin to lose our natural immunities to life's dangers.
- I do not know how many hundreds of thousands of years the human species has lived and survived on the earth. I do know that as humans became hunter-gatherers and then farmers, herders, and fishermen, they learned to return to the earth gratitude for their food, shelter, and their very existence.
- Seeds from crops were replanted, smaller fish were returned to the sea, and little birds and creatures were protected so they could grow.
- Man established an honoring, a gift-giving back to the natural world he inhabited. Instinctually he knew the give and take of survival. It was part of his human nature.
- Gift-giving is a huge part of human nature because of reciprocity. The earth gives to me. I give to the Earth. It is a renewing cycle—give, take, reap, plant, seed, birth, death—the passing forward to an afterlife, just as a newborn is being delivered in another village.

- Gift-giving is also a way a species can honor and classify its priorities. By giving a gift we mean to start or continue a relationship, we are saying, "You are important."
- When the ancient humans gave offerings to their departed, their image-Gods, their animus spirits, they were acknowledging the perpetuity of their species.
- The ancients were "gift-thankers," as are modern-day generous human beings, who appreciate and value the legacy of generosity.

Quotes: Some Negative Traits of Human Nature

- Damaged people damage everyone around them.
- All that an evil person needs to triumph is for a good person to do nothing.
- Some humans think they know everything about everything, but in reality, they know nothing about anything.
- A victim never has to defend or criticize himself, once he decides he is a victim.
- Victim mentality is very slippery. It reasons, "If I am a victim, I need no limits, no moral evaluation of my actions. Why should I? I'm the victim."
- Emotions are triggers.
- It is easy to say things. It is hard to put them into practice.
- Respond to nature as part of yourself—not as a stranger or something to be exploited.
- Refuse to participate in waste, greed, or exploitation. That is a moral choice. That choice is what makes you a good human being.

CHAPTER 13

Indigenia-Aborgina

Words matter. Language matters. People and places matter. Why? Because they define us and because they explain who we are.

"Native" American peoples, "indigenous," "tribal," "aboriginal" define how man and community began on this earth.

Latin, the prime source for English speakers, gives meaning to people born of the land. Let me give you some examples:

1	Native	Meaning "born of" or in Latin, "natal"
2	Indigenous	Meaning "originating naturally in a special place" or in Latin, "indigena" or "native"
3	Tribal	Adjective describing people living under one chief or leader, sharing a common ancestry, language, and culture or in Latin, "tribus" or "group"
4	Aboriginal	Meaning "from the beginning" or in Latin "origo" meaning "to rise" or "existing from the beginning"

Of course, Latin word origins do not cover most of the world's population. But the concept of indigenous peoples, living in tribal cultures, native to their lands and countries, is universal.

For me, an Italian-American, Latin works perfectly. I can roll the syllables of Indigena (originating, in a natural place) or Aborigina (existing from the beginning, the origin) off my tongue and it sounds totally Italian!

This is where my story begins.

When I was growing up in Ithaca, New York, my playgrounds were hills, lakes, waterfalls, creeks, orchards, forest trails, hilltop gazing of clouds and birds, seasonal physical games on ice, in ponds, gathering wildflowers, arrowheads, lucky stones, picking apples, snowshoeing in the backyard, watching geese fly away in October and return in May. My world was native and rustic.

My home was a sacred place to our family. Our parents ruled the roost. We obeyed, we disobeyed, and we laughed, shouted, cried, and played together. Our meals were important times for family connecting, to talk, to argue, to tease, to embrace each other, to love each other. We were a tribal unit inside our home.

Outside our home, life was different. We did not associate much with neighbors or others, because our "Italian-ness" set us apart in this community. My early years were spent in ignorance of white vs. indigenous mentalities. For me, everything in my world was inside of me already.

One day, when I was seven years old, I was with my Brownie troop. We were talking about Native American Indians, and how our part of New York state's Finger Lakes was historically Indian land.

As my Brownie leader was telling us about the Mohawks, Senecas, Iroquois, and Cayuga Indian tribes, I was so happy. I was hearing about how they lived, what they ate, how they traveled on the land and water, and how they believed in creation and the creatures, living things, plants, bird, and clouds.

I raised my hand excitedly when she asked if we had any questions or anything we wanted to say.

"Yes!" I exclaimed, "I am an Indian girl!" I proudly happily declared.

I remember this as though it was yesterday. "Now, Nancy, how can you say that?" she asked. "You are what we call, Caucasian, which means white-skinned people. Indians have red skin."

"Oh, but I have long black shiny hair!" I responded proudly. I am an Italian Indian."

Now, almost seventy years later, I feel the exact same way. My childhood understanding of the world around me was based on home—nature and identity born of tradition and respect for customs, beliefs, and attitudes. My identity has always been an indigenous one. I was nurtured, loved, taught, and embraced by parents who taught my sister and brother and me what it meant to be a good human being.

They encouraged us to develop our abilities, so we could grow in joy and pride. They showed us that "Home" is never outside of you and that you carry it wherever you go, and home is where your heart is happy.

That message to us in my childhood was prescient, it had prophecy in it. Little did my parents know that I would be a rebellious, strong-headed young woman who would journey to far places, away from them, and my childhood home, but would always return.

This chapter isn't about me. It is about Native American life and Indigenous peoples. I'll just tell you that in my travels, and my returns, and more travels, I have encountered Navaho, Hopi, and Zuni cultures, ancient Greek and Mid-eastern cultures, Latin American cultures, Celtic and Norman cultures, Caribbean cultures, Eastern European and Slavic cultures, Russian cultures and Scandinavian cultures.

My only regret is that I won't see Tibetan culture prior to China's takeover, nor will I fulfill two dreams: one to go to Mongolia and the other to the hill country of Japan!

I am happiest near the sea, the mountains, and where they meet.

What is it about an Indigenous future that so captures my heart and soul? First and foremost is the spirituality and the wisdom that accompanies the beliefs of Creation and the philosophies for living on this earth.

I am an ignorant bystander for Native American life. Especially now, in our nation, Native American people are standing once again for the right to be who they are, to protect their culture, and their heritage, and to fight for the precious Earth they so revere.

My personality is who I am. My understanding of the personality of Native American culture comes from reading many of their famous authors and numerous historical works describing Indian history in North America.

I encourage you to find your own readings and I will give you some references in the bibliography, but believe me you can spend a lifetime learning what Native Americans have known for centuries. Let's start anyway! Ready?

Creation Story

Ancient Seneca Indian Story of Creation

The two-leggeds came from the Water Nursery of Creation and stood on the shore. They were called humans. They would be no greater or lesser than any of the Great Mysteries of other tribes or clans.

There were Earth People and Sky People among the two-legged tribes. The Sky People came from the pure

intellect and the omnipotent mind of Great Mystery. Some had chosen to leave the tribes of Thunder, Clouds, Stars, and Moons to experience the limitations of being physical.

These Sky People had chosen to receive hearts and bodies and learn through the limitations of being human.

The Earth People of the two-legged tribe were no less courageous in their missions because they were to learn the Lessons of Harmony with all other life-forms on the Planet.

These beautiful Earth and Sky People of the two-legged tribe were guardians of the Sacred Hoop and the Planetary Family. It was their mission to keep the heart-fire of the external Flame burning brightly throughout all seven Worlds of Time.

The changes that would occur during those eons would shape the destiny of Mother Earth and all her children.

The Seven Worlds

Ancient Seneca Indian Creation Story

The Spirit World Itself
The First World of Love
The Second World of Ice
The Third World of Water
The Fourth World of Separation
The Fifth World of Illumination
The Sixth World of Prophecy and Revelation
The Seventh World of Completion

Creation Story

Told by Black Elk, Holy Man of the Oglala Sioux

I was standing on the highest mountain of all and around about beneath me was the Hoop of the World. While I stood there I saw more than I can tell and I understood more than I saw. I was seeing in a sacred manner the shapes of all things in the Spirit and the shapes of all shapes as they must live together, like One Being.

I saw the Sacred Hoop of my people was one of many Hoops that made one circle as wide as Daylight and as Starlight and in the center grew one mighty Flowering Cree to shelter all the children of One Mother and One Father.

And I saw that it was Holy.

Then a Voice said, "Behold this day for it is yours to make. Now you stand upon the Center of the Earth.

Black Elk

B.1860 – 1953

Storytelling and Native Wisdom and the White Man

When asked by an anthropologist what the Indians called American before the white man came, an Indian said simply, "Ours."

In the 19th century, when the federal government wrenched Native People from their homelands, forcing them on long desperate marches, they took children, heritage, and hope away from the Indians.

To the white man, capital, property, real-estate, and resources like oil and gold were a vision of an amazing future the Indian lands would provide.

To the Indians, the land was everything: identity, connection to ancestors, home to beloved animals and creatures, and the source of their ancient identity. Their lands connected the American Indians to the Universe, to Life itself. The land was sacred, as the land was where the people enacted their responsibilities, first to Mother Earth, second to the Sacred Gods, and third to the Human Race.

What the white man couldn't predict because of their ignorance of Native Culture was that Native Peoples keep their stories alive. Tribal leaders, holy men, rituals and storytellers have to this very day kept Native Wisdom alive.

Native Americans keep things alive with their language that describes all living things as just that … living.

Things are not just objects or silent to Indians, as they are to the white man. The Indian hears the voices of his world all the time. All living creatures and natural events intermingle in Native language with wisdoms and lessons.

Indian speakers who now are trying to keep Native languages from becoming extinct call their words "the grammar of animacy." The Living World is never an "it" or a "thing." The Native American uses the same words they use for family to address their Living World. Words like "grandmother, grandfather, mother, sister, brother, great-uncle, friend."

Storyteller, teachers, and tribal leaders know that words, music, dance, and art are the language of their world. It is how their stories stay alive. Holy men of the tribes have visions that show them lessons and truth.

Here are quotes, passages, and narratives that reveal how Native peoples speak to Nature and to each other. Their Wisdom and Philosophy, their guidelines for human behavior and citizenship, and their love of Nature are flawless testaments to the best of human endeavors on this earth.

Citizenship

Citizenship meant the following: allegiance, alliances, responsibilities in financial, civic education and infrastructural areas of life, loyalties, caretaking for community, shared beliefs and language, protecting family, village, tribe, and nation from political action and outside engagers.

Twylah Nitsch – Seneca Elder

Gratitude

They were wise enough to be grateful.

Humans who lived with respect, gratitude, and humility lived right in the world.

We must reciprocate for the generosity of the earth with gratitude.

Mayan Sacred Text Popol Vuh
and Oral Tradition

Gratitude, bravery, generosity, integrity and endurance are fundamental virtues.

Blue Horse of the Oglala Lakota Tribe
1822 - 1908

Wisdom

The seven talents of wisdom are Faith, Love, Intuition, Will, Creativity, Magnetism and Healing.

Seneca Indian Creation Story

What I know was given to me for men and it is true and beautiful.

The thoughts of men should rise as high as eagles.

Black Elk, Sioux Holy Man

It is hard to follow one great vision in this world of darkness and many changing shadows among those shadows one may get lost.

Black Elk, Sioux Holy Man

It is from understanding that wisdom and power come.

Lakota Saying

I am an old man waiting for yesterday while looking for tomorrow's promise, remembering when I was still young and could hope. But when I see each morning star, I see wisdom.

Lakota Saying

Prayer

When I die I go up where the Spirit goes, into the sky.

Crazy Horse
Sioux Warrior 19ᵗʰ C.

Humans get meaning and power from the life forms of the entire universe. A system of relationships and prayer invokes those relationships.

Lakota Saying

Pray to the great Mystery dwelling inside the Eternal Flame.

Seneca Saying

Nature

Did you know that trees talk? Well, they do. They talk to each other and they will talk to you if you listen. Trouble is: white people don't listen. They never learned to listen to the Indians so I don't suppose they will listen to other voices in nature. But I have learned a lot from trees. Sometimes about the weather, sometimes about animals, sometimes about the Great Spirit.

Walking Buffalo – Canadian Stoney Indian Chief
1872 – 1944

Hummingbirds are healers who bring luck and love to those they visit. They lead from here to there the thoughts of men. If someone intends good to you, the humming bird takes that desire to you all the way.

Ancient Aztec Saying

We did not think of the great open plains, the beautiful rolling hills and winding streams with tangled growth as "wild." Only to white men was nature a "wilderness." Only to him was the land "infested" with "wild" animals and "savage" people.

To us the Earth was tamed and beautiful. We were surrounded with the blessings of the Great Mystery. The "Wildness" began when our land was invaded. Our love for the forest and hills and our care for our trees and plants and animals never left our hearts or spirits even as the white man approached to "tame" the Wild West.

Chief Luther Standing Bear
Oglala Lakota Chief

"The Great Spirit, the Sacred Divine, the Great Mystery, Animals, Music, Clouds, Flowers, Foods, Plants, Vegetables, Birds, Wisdom"

"Wakan Tanka," Lakota Saying

Animals and plants are taught by Wakan Tanka what they are to do. Wakan Tanka teaches the birds to make nests, yet the nests of all birds are not alike. Wakan Tanka gives them merely the outline. Some make better nests than others.

Some animals are satisfied with very rough dwellings while others make attractive places in which to live.

Some animals take better care of their young than others. The forest is the home of many birds and animals and the water is the home of fish and reptiles.

All birds, even those of the same species, are not alike. It is the same with animals and plants and human beings.

Wakan Tanka does not make two birds or two trees or two horses or two humans alike, because each one is placed here by him to be an independent individuality and to rely upon itself.

Okute, Teton Sioux

Many indigenous people share the understanding that we are each endowed with a particular gift, a unique ability. Birds sing, stars glitter. It is understood that these gifts have a dual nature: a gift is also a responsibility. The birds' gift is song. Then it has a responsibility to greet the day with music. Their duty is to sing and we receive the song as a gift.

What is our gift? What is our responsibility? How shall we use them? People who know they have gifts and are aware of their responsibility to the Earth and to human life have words. Other beings can fly, see at night, rip open trees with their claws, make maple syrup. Humans may not have wings or leaves, but we have language as our gift and our responsibility.

Writing is an art of reciprocity with the living land for me. Words to remember old stories, words to tell new stories, stories that bring science and spirit back together to nurture our becoming.

Robin Wall Kimmerer
Potawatomi Indian,
scientist, professor, author

Introduction

Council Fires of the Ancients

In ancient times, the main purpose of nightly Council Fires for the people was to learn how to listen. The truths of how to live in harmony were kept alive by wise storytellers who would relate tribal wisdom through medicine stories as those who gathered to listen sat around the fires. Tribal traditions, history, acts of courage, and lessons on how to discover the true self came to life through the events related in the legends of the Ancestors. It was the responsibility of the listeners to relate and apply those truths to their personal lives in a manner that would make them grow.

As the authors of this book, we are storytellers. The responsibility of sharing the voices of our Teachers has fallen to us. Our Teachers have been our own Ancestors, our Totems, the Spirits of the Wind, and All Our Relations in the Planetary Family. This particular story is the history of the Creation of Our Planetary Mother and her children as it was passed down through Native Elders and as it was experienced firsthand by the seven-sided Medicine Stone, Geeh

Yuk (Seven Talents). The content of Seven Talents' story may startle some people who do not know the history of the Earth from one of the Native viewpoints.

Nyahweh Scanoh, greetings, Children of Earth. My ancient eyes have long beheld our Earth Mother, and many long winters have been carried on my back. Since before the dawn of Creation I have traveled through the Void discovering and rediscovering the beauty of the Great Mystery. Wise I have become, and yet each new change in the Planetary Family continues to allow my understanding to grow further, as if I were a newborn babe. Before the creation of our physical world, I was innocent and yet hungry to know the mysteries of life. I have recorded each change completed and lesson learned along the Path of Beauty in order to mark the growth of all life-forms.

I have soared with Eagle high above the canyons of time observing the evolution of the Planetary Family. You and I are alike in many ways. Though you are human and I am a Stone Person, we both feel through our hearts. We both learn through experiences shared with All Our Relations. Every relation has personal missions to complete so that life abundant may flourish and grow. I have been a teacher and friend to many two-legged humans, teaching them the similarities among all members of the Planetary Family.

I am the oldest of Earth Tribes, the Stone People. Our Earth-forged bodies have been fashioned from the erupting heat of volcanic creation and the ice-blue cold that tempers our ancient spirits. *The remembering* of each tempered spirit, set in stone, allows us to hold the memories and records of all that has ever occurred in this world. From other Stone People, who have fallen from the Great Star Nation, we have learned much of other galaxies. The Meteorites who have joined us from the stars have added to our knowledge and to the libraries carried within our rock bodies. We have many stories to tell the Children of Earth about the worlds that came before the written histories of the two-legged humans.

I have waited until now, the dawning of this Fifth World of Peace, to set these stories in motion. I am called Geeh Yuk, or Seven Talents, in one of your Native American languages. I have come to teach you how the Language of the Stones came to be and to bring forth these ancient *rememberings*.

Those of you who have ears to hear and eyes to see and hearts to understand know that these truths are for all races, all people. The Great Mystery created the Children of Earth in different colors so that one day they would come together and compose the Whirling Rainbow Tribe of Peace. Now is the dawning of that special time. The promise of world peace is unfolding. We, of the Stone Tribe, trust that the Path of Beauty will be made clear to all two-leggeds once they remember the victories and the failures of the other worlds that flourished and then passed into oblivion. Those old worlds have served the Children of Earth by leaving the legacies that gently point the way to the new world's prophecy of peace. We, your ancient Brothers and Sisters of the Stone Tribe, are here to remind you that the time is now and that the power of this prophecy lies in you.

THE WAY OF LOVE,
THE WAY OF LIFE
There are many things
that might help us walk
the Way of Love.
The words below come from the
ancient wisdom tradition
of a North American People
in southern Mexico.
They are reproduced for us
in a book by Don Miguel Ruiz called
The Four Agreements.

Be impeccable with your word.
Speak with integrity.
Say only what you mean.
Avoid using the word to
speak against yourself
or to gossip about others.
Use the power of your word
in the direction of truth and love.

Don't take anything personally.
Nothing others do is because of you.
What others say and do is a projection
of their own reality, their own dream.
When you are immune
to the opinions and actions of others
you won't be the victim
of needless suffering.

Don't make assumptions.
Find the courage to ask questions
and to express what you really want.
Communicate with others
as clearly as you can
to avoid misunderstandings,

sadness and drama.
With just this one agreement,
you can completely transform your life.

Always do your best.
Your best is going to change
from moment to moment.
It will be different when you are healthy
as opposed to sick.
Under any circumstances,
simply do your best
and you will avoid self-judgment,
self-abuse and regret.

A SENECA PRAISE

Oh Great Mystery, we awake
To another sun
Grateful for the gifts bestowed
Granted one by one—
Grateful for the greatest gift,
The precious breath of life;
Grateful for abilities
That guide us day and night.

As we walk our chosen paths
Of lessons we must learn—
Spiritual peace and happiness
Rewards of life we earn.
Thank you for your Spiritual Strength
And for our thoughts to praise;
Thank you for your Infinite Love
That guides us through these days.

♥

CHAPTER 14

The Healing Power of Music, Art, and Writing

*I*t happens to all of us. We hear a song, a rhythm beating, a joyous drumbeat, a sweet melody, an inspiring crescendo and we respond!

We sway, we clap, we sing along, we tap our fingers, we dance, we raise our arms up and sway with eyes shut. We are inspired, we are in the present moment, and we are one with this unseen force of creation that simply said, removes care and erases sorrow, replacing them with pure happiness.

When we see a painting, read a poem, finish a novel, or hear a lecture that inspires us, something unseen "clicks" inside of us, filling us with happiness and stimulating us in a good way.

When we hold a pen in our hand and enter a diary page or write a story or a poem, our minds carry our thoughts through our fingers, releasing energy as we touch our thoughts to paper.

I've always felt joy, inspiration and a certain calm peace when I write. I feel a flowing release of parts of myself that I wasn't aware were inside me.

When I play Mozart or a gospel hymn, or a love song on the piano, I can feel a strong impulse from inside my chest. It wants to burst into the world in joy and power. If it is sad music with melancholy truths, I know somewhere, somehow I am connecting to a force, unknown, unseen, which is holding me in its arms.

When I paint a picture or draw a tiny intricate pattern with a fine noble pen, the communication streaming into my fingers, the feeling of creating in the same rhythm as my breathing is extraordinary.

The physical, the visual—from where does it come? Healer of Happiness.

We have been creative beings since the beginning of our human existence. I am not a scientist and I know nothing, but I have to assume that as a species, we have used materials all around us to express ourselves.

I am focusing here on the healing aspects of music, art and writing. I do, however, honor that the same impulses used to inspire are also used to destroy—a war drumbeat is not about peace. A beautifully carved knife or spear is not meant to inspire joy. An edict of war is not going to produce sweet comfort to its reader.

I instead think of early man, with his rituals of dancing and his basic instruments of bone, stringed wood, carved flutes. I see him dancing to drum beats, hand claps, and vocal praises.

Why? Why did these impulses exist in the beginning of our earthly lives? I think it is because our brains have been "wired" from the beginning to respond to cues and clues around us.

From the onset of man living in groups, music has soothed and entertained. There has been art on cave walls since the beginning. There have been scratches on stones and walls, telling stories all around the world.

Ancient peoples, just like us, received pleasure and felt something larger than themselves when they were creative. It is basic philosophy to accept that the five senses are what connect us to the world: hearing, vision, touch, smell and taste. Those are neurologic truths.

But how and why we respond to music, art, writing (and other creative arts not discussed here, such as dance, cuisine, dramatic performance) must have some answers.

The answers are coming. In the past twenty years, the study of the human brain and the neuroscience of human feeling, activity and function have blossomed into a vibrant and exciting field of inquiry.

When I was a nursing student in the 1960s, we studied the human brain from afar. In those days, dissections, x-rays, MRIs, cat scans didn't apply to neurology.

We studied diseases and behaviors associated with the brain, but that's where it ended. Neurosurgeons performed surgeries to correct anatomy or anomalies. Psychiatrists dealt with behavioral issues, while mental hospitals dealt with obvious illness. We did not have the tools to discover the "whys" of brain function.

Now we do.

In December 2007, an article was published in the *Journal of Critical Care Medicine*. I have kept the *New York Times* articles describing the study on my piano with my music.

In short, a surgeon, Dr. Claudius Conrad, has published a study he and his colleagues made connecting music to healing. Dr. Conrad studied piano from the age of five, excelling to the level of concert pianist. Not only was he a Harvard Medical School trained surgeon, he also holds a doctorate in stem cell biology and a second doctorate in music philosophy. This man is a rare gem. His talents, education, and training reinforce his own life, so that he works better in the operating room when he listens to music.

He also knows, through his own experience and studies published, that music can facilitate patients by bringing down blood pressure, pain levels and heart rates. Music seems to stimulate hormones produced in the brain that are traditionally associated with stress reduction.

Dr. Conrad and his associates discovered that patients recovering in intensive care units from surgeries who were given headphones with Mozart's music produced a fifty-percent jump in the presence of a pituitary growth hormone, P6H as it is known is a growth hormone that helps the body respond to immune system threats and promotes healing.

Dr. Conrad, himself an extraordinary combination of surgeon, pianist, and scientist, sees the human body responding to music in ways never described.

Music heals, art inspires, and writing uses hand-brain coordination. Artists using tools in caves or elegant brushes in their modern studios are tapping into a mystery.

We may respond to joyous music, weep at a tragic aria, or stand for hours before a painting. Why? How?

For me, I am happy with what I know. Sometimes, when I'm playing a passage in a Mozart sonata, my heart feels really full and happy and a voice from my soul says, "I am here." I smile, knowing I feel better having touched the Spirit of Life.

NEW YORK TIMES / C.J. GUNTHER

Claudius Conrad, a surgeon with Massachusetts General Hospital, plays the piano at the Steinert Hall at Steinert and Sons in Boston.

> "I think he composed music the way he did partly because it made him feel better."
>
> **DR. CLAUDIUS CONRAD,**
> who has studied the possible healing effect of Mozart's music

as a sniper in the German Army's mountain corps, where his commander found every opportunity to fly him out of the Alps for some piano time.

After his service he decided to pursue medicine while continuing to study music. He earned a bachelor's degree at the University of Munich and then, more or less simulta-neously, two doctorates and a medical degree.

Conrad's music dissertation examined why and how Mozart's music seemed to ease the pain of intensive-care patients.

He concentrated not on physiological mechanisms but on mechanisms within Mozart's music.

"It is still a controversial idea," he said recently, "wheth-er Mozart has more of this sort

ers. But as a musician I wanted to look at how it might."

Conrad noted that Mozart used distinctive phrases that are fairly short, often only four or even two measures long, and then repeated these phras-es to build larger sections. Yet he changed these figures often in ways the listener may not notice — a change in left-hand arpeggios or chord structures, for instance, that slips by unre-marked while the ear attends the right hand's melody, which itself may be slightly embel-lished.

These intricate variations are absorbed as part of a me-lodic accessibility so well organized that even a sonata for two pianos never feels crowded in the ear, even when it grows dense on the page. The melody lulls and delights while the underlying complexi-ty stimulates.

But even if this explains the music's power to stimulate and relax, "an obvious ques-tion that comes up," Conrad said, "is why Mozart would write music that is so sooth-ing."

Mozart's letters and biogra-phies, Conrad said, portray a man almost constantly sick, constantly fending off one infection or ailment after an-other.

"Whether he did it intention-ally or not," Conrad said, "I think he composed music the way he did partly because it made him feel better."

Recently, Conrad has fo-cused on specific mechanisms that may help explain music's effects on the body.

In a paper published last December in the journal Criti-cal Care Medicine, he and colleagues revealed an unex-pected element in distressed

sponse to music: a jump in pituitary growth hormone, which is known to be crucial in healing.

"It's a sort of quickening," he said, "that produces a calm-ing effect." Accelerando pro-duces tranquillo.

The study itself was fairly simple. The researchers fitted 10 postsurgical intensive-care patients with headphones, and in the hour just after the pa-tients' sedation was lifted, five were treated to gentle Mozart piano music while five heard nothing.

The patients listening to music showed several respons es that Conrad expected, based on other studies: re-duced blood pressure and heart rate, less need for pain medication and a 20 percent drop in two important stress hormones, epinephrine and interleukin-6, or IL-6. Amid these expected responses was the study's new finding: a 50 percent jump in pituitary growth hormone.

No one conducting these studies had yet measured growth hormone, whose wor includes driving growth, re-sponding to threats to the immune system and promot-ing healing. Conrad included was because research over th last five years has shown that growth hormone generally rises with stress and falls wit relaxation.

"This means you would expect GH, like epinephrine and IL-6, to go down in this case," Morley, of St. Louis University, said of growth hormone. "Yet here it goes The question is whether the jump in growth hormone actually drives the sedative effect or is part of somethin else going on."

For Conrad, the finding offers a sort of scientifico-m sical elegance: Here, it seem may be a hormonal parallel music's power to simulta-neously rouse and soothe.

Conrad said he hopes to expand his study of music's effects on growth hormone intensive-care patients. He also planning roughly simil studies of how music affect surgeon's performance.

SCIENCE JOURNAL

HE POWER OF MUSIC to soothe and even heal the human body as been well documented. But a pianist-surgeon has gone a step irther — to explore the ways in which listening to Mozart after urgery actually may stimulate the growth of new tissue in ntensive care patients.

Music's charms could also be a potent cure

and the sea...

By DAVID DOBBS
THE NEW YORK TIMES

For Claudius Conrad, a 30-year-old surgeon who has played the piano seriously since he was 5, music and medicine are entwined — from the academic realm down to the level of the fine-fingered dexterity required at the piano bench and the operating table.

"If I don't play for a couple of days," said Conrad, a third-year surgical resident at Harvard Medical School who also holds doctorates in stem cell biology and music philosophy, "I cannot feel things as well in surgery. My hands are not as tender with the tissue. They are not as sensitive to the feedback that the tissue gives you."

Like many surgeons, Conrad says he works better when he listens to music. And he cites studies, including some of his own, showing that music is helpful to patients as well — bringing relaxation and reducing blood pressure, heart rate, stress hormones, pain and the need for pain medication.

But to the extent that music heals, how does it heal? The

underlying mechanism has moved slowly. Now Conrad is trying to change that. He recently published a provocative paper suggesting that music may exert healing and sedative effects partly through a paradoxical stimulation of a growth hormone generally associated with stress rather than healing.

This jump in growth hormone, said Dr. John Morley, an endocrinologist at St. Louis University Medical Center who was not involved with the study, "is not what you'd expect, and it's not precisely clear what it means."

But he said it raised "some wonderful new possibilities about the physiology of healing," and added: "And of course it has a nice sort of metaphorical ring. We used to talk about the neuroendocrine system being a sort of neuronal orchestra conductor directing the immune system. Here we have music stimulating this conductor to get the healing process started."

Born in Munich, Conrad took up the piano when he was 5 and trained in elite music schools in Munich, Augs-

If you trace these notes
as though they were a rhythm
strip from an ECG (heart tracing)
they match!

<u>Santo</u> — (Argentine liturgical text)

Santo, Santo, santo, mi corazon
te adora! Mi corazon te sabe decir
santo eré Señor.

Ho - ly, ho - ly, ho- ly, my heart, my heart a-dores you!

My heart pours out my praise to_ you; you are ho - ly, Lord.

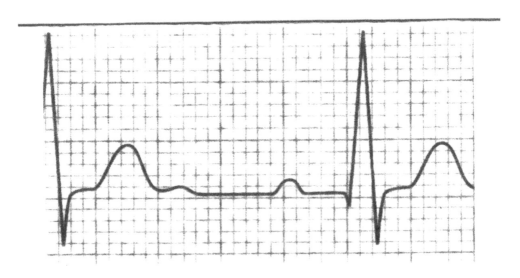

this peace sedates me.

Peace before us

1. Peace be-fore us, peace be-hind us,
2. Love be-fore us, love be-hind us,
3. Light be-fore us, light be-hind us,
4. Christ be-fore us, Christ be-hind us,

peace un-der our feet. _____ Peace with-in us,
love un-der our feet. _____ Love with-in us,
light un-der our feet. _____ Light with-in us,
Christ un-der our feet. _____ Christ with-in us,

1, 2, 3, 4, 5.

peace o-ver us, let all a-round us be peace. _____
love o-ver us, let all a-round us be love. _____
light o-ver us, let all a-round us be light. _____
Christ o-ver us, let all a-round us be Christ. _____

CHAPTER 15

The Mystery of History

I was born in 1946.

One day not long ago I was browsing in a furniture store. As I walked around the vast array of merchandise, I came upon a section of chairs, tables, sofas, lamps and accessories that looked like someone had gone into the home I grew up in and transported my childhood, adolescence and married years into the store!

A friendly saleswoman approached me. "Isn't this the most beautiful collection of 'mid-late–century' furniture you have ever seen?"

"Excuse me?" I asked. I didn't understand what she was saying.

"Mid-late-century," she replied, "you know, the 1950s."

"Oh," I said, as something shifting inside my brain prompted my next words, "Well, this furniture is what I grew up with and still possess much of it. I never thought of myself as being labeled 'mid-late-century'!"

And so we arrive at a gate, we open the gate and step into history.

I have spent much of my life learning about peoples and cultures of times past. From my childhood I gathered stories of Native American history as I was fascinated by arrowheads and old Indian burial mounds in my part of upstate New York.

I have studied ancient wisdom for as long as I can remember—Greek, Asian, Persian, Chinese, Aztec, Celtic, Hebrew, Muslim, and Christian writers have transported me thorough centuries back into their worlds.

I have visited museums of primeval history, seen ancient walls and ruins, stood on rocky cliffs looking at seas once travelled thousands of years ago by humans.

I have collected stones from European castle walls. I have read fables and stories all ending in the deep truths of passing time.

I have always understood their meanings, these words of ancient peoples. I often nod in agreement when I'm reading a quote from Confucius. I close my eyes and picture a battle scene described by Herodotus. I understand deep in my heart and soul what these two men, born 2600 years ago were writing about.

If I read modern history, defined by myself only as events of the last five-hundred years, I am more discouraged than enlightened, for I see a reworking of the narrative of preceding centuries. I sense a manipulation of earlier topics so the accomplishments of the Renaissance or the Enlightenment become the victory of man. I perceive the beginning of what I see in today's world, and that is an arrogant dismissal of old furniture so newer models can be sold as the real thing.

How many times have you heard the phrase, "History repeats itself?" How many times have you read or heard someone declare that because we don't know the past, we can't possibly prevent making mistakes in the present.

History is a topic. Time is what teaches us. It is ironic that today we have experts in all fields of our lives—science, math, ecology, industry, world politics—who opine, teach, preach, write, speak (often shout) what they know to be the absolute truth.

History is a topic. Truth isn't a topic. Just because we now have technological prowess to move mountains does not mean we respect or understand these mountains.

So, I am left with a simple awareness that the thousands of years of human wisdoms, truths, artwork, architecture, and yes, war are always with us. The only thing in human existence that has changed is the way Truth and Wisdom are communicated.

Here is a question for you … how is it that I can read a passage from the Talmud that came into use in the Middle Ages (beginning in the fifth century after Christ), which says exactly the same thing, teaches precisely the same lesson as Socrates (five centuries before Christ)?

Or another question … was the physical world so accessible to these ancient souls that they could describe stars, planets, the origins of life, the ways of family or clan, and the needs and moods of the seasons each in their own environments? That setting widely differs from desert caves, high cliffs of northern Scotland, deep glens and mountain peaks of Greece, arid lands of Egypt, all the way to the bamboo forests of deep China.

The "physicalness" of the Ancient World places these ancient humans directly in and among the truths of their lives.

So, they wrote about those truths. They imagined those truths and throughout the passage of time they bequeathed their knowledge, their conclusions, their parables, their warnings, and their tips for practical living that often meant survival.

They had rituals. They had academics. They had their own language and writing techniques. They knew what they knew, and they dreamed and thought about what they didn't know.

They asked questions, leaving many unanswered. They confronted mystery as spirit or imagination and wove it into their daily lives.

The ancient peoples and their millennial descendants, including you and me, knew that a life past the mortal episode they were living existed.

War was a part of their world. From Persian invasions, to Genghis Khan, to the Crusaders, to World War II, war has been an historical truth.

That truth includes love, art, music, dance and theater, as well as farming, fishing, hunting, spiritual devotion, homemaking, and travel.

I read the same teachings of the Native Iroquois as the beginning of the world that I read in the Old Testament. I read the same dire warnings of Aristotle as the Samurai warriors of 14th Century Japan.

I read the same herbal and medicinal remedy texts from ancient India and current-day homeotherapists.

"The more things change, the more they stay the same."

What stays the same? Basic human nature, our instincts for survival and procreation; our need for connection to other in groups, be they families, tribes, clans, nations, or regiments; our need to be heard and respected and listened to with authentic attention; our need to grieve, our need to embrace; our need to give and take, our need to teach and to improve the lives of our children; our need for comfort, security and safety; our need for entertainment and laughter; our need to remember those gone before us and those we will leave behind.

History is us. Now. Then. In the future. History is stories, fables, myths. History is hard to learn when war and human suffering is described.

History is a wondrous gift for our imaginations. History is time travel. We need to look at Time.

CHAPTER 16

Time

I'm sitting at my desk. As I write I see a sparkle from my wedding ring as it catches a morning sunbeam. I look at the diamond.

It was my husband's grandmother's diamond, passed down to me, a South African gem. I look at it. "How old are you?" I ask.

It must be thousands of years old, maybe hundreds of thousands of years! I touch my ear with my hand and feel the pearl earring I put on this morning.

"How old are you and which ocean did you come from?"

Time fascinates me. I truly believe that time is all we will ever question.

Attached to this chapter is something I wrote during the COVID epidemic. It was, and still is, a way of time being seen, felt and lived that differed from any experience I ever had.

Time seemed to sink downward.

We can't explain our existence on this earth without asking about time. Unlike physicists and philosophers, historians and storytellers, I don't have a lot of answers—I do have observations.

It seems that as the human race became more sophisticated, the measurement of days, months, years changed from natural simple tools like measuring a summer solstice or watching a crop grow to maturity and matching those events to some sort of sundial, calendar, hourglass, or sky-watching device to more formal instruments.

Soon man had dates, and years, minutes, seconds and decades to mark the passage of human life, we began to look at history as eras, or decades, or ages describing not the actual flow of reality, but describing man's accomplishments.

Man began to use time as though it were a possession, an employee, a means to an end.

Humans invented clocks and "time" tables, schedules and events marking the passage of something, the observation of something they wanted to remember.

Time is not an instrument. I have had a lot of time to think about life, I have been lucky enough to have enough hours to myself that I'm not marching in minutes but in quiet contemplation, reading or walking in nature. I don't watch anything or care about schedules. I'm living in the moment.

Maybe that's what it's all about. Some days seem slow and others fly by. Our lives are mere "seconds" in the universe's clock.

So why doesn't man respect and honor Time? Why isn't Time placed high above money, pleasure or self?

I think it is because each of us deep down in the very core of the very core of our souls know the truth. Time is all we have as human beings. Our actions will determine our respect and humbleness before it, but Time is the greatest force in our lives. That is why Time needs to be met every morning with Love. It's all we have.

Life means a true waiting, a true preparation for a journey past our human bodies, our ancient history as humans into a place of eternity.

Time teaches us to wait. It humbles us.

It's Time to Get Started

What time do you have?
Another time, another place.
You pick the time.
Time is on my mind.
Time flies.
Time lays heavy on my hands.
Well, it's about time.
Time is on my mind.
If I could put time in a bottle.
What time is it?
Next time it's on you.
There's no time like the present.
If only I had the time.
The last time we did this …
Take your time, we have all day.
This isn't a good time right now.
Last time we did this I was five.
It's time to go now.

What is Time?
Where does it come from and where does it go?
Does Time need a conscious observer? Is it like "If a tree falls in the forest and no one is there, does it make a sound?"
If Time passes does it need to be observed?
Can Time go backwards?
Can Time go underneath or above?
Does Time flow or sink or bubble up or scatter?
Is Time short or long?
Is there anywhere in any universe where Time isn't, or hasn't been or won't be?

Will Time ever stop?
If Time stops can it begin again?
Can Time be remembered?
Why is it called Time?
Humans invented clocks, Time didn't.
Before clocks how did early man know Time other than daylight and darkness?
How do we talk about time, as a noun, a proper noun, an adjective, a verb?

Does Time have energy?

Does Time have sound?

Does Time have motion?

Does time have shape?

Does time have emotion or conscious awareness?

Does Time have gender or form? A god or goddess, a monster, an angel, a rose, a cloud, a sunset?

Is Time sacred?

Who gave Time to the human race and to all living things?

Do dead things know about Time?

Does time talk to Life, or to Sorrow or to Happiness or to Wisdom?

We have weather forecasts and timelines for natural events. Are they prophecies? Or truths?

Who will teach us about Time and how do we do that? Will we ask the right questions? Will we accept the answers?

Does Time-knowledge change in a human's lifetime?

Does Time need Experience to recognize and accept it?

Does Time have a personality? Is it in control or easily molded?

What words, in any language, speak of time? Words like now, never, yesterday, tomorrow, remember when? I forget, too late, too early, last year, next year, centuries ago.

Almanacs, Astronomy, Physics, Astrophysics, Literature, Art, Music, Poetry, Religions, Spiritual Life and Holy documents, Engineering, Medicine, Science, Culinary Science, and on and on and on to what??? Infinity ??????

CHAPTER 17

Borrowed Lives and the Ten Gifts of Love

*H*omes are living things. So are the hopes and dreams within them. Mother, Father, Sister, Brother, Son, Daughter, all lives gifted to us, all lives borrowed from and blended into one another.

Human beings desire connection. We are not meant for isolation and we realize our finest selves within relationship. Family is all the gift we will ever need.

What is the gift? Simply stated, it is Love. The parenting and caring for others, the learnings of human behaviors, the teaching, preaching, disciplining, rewarding, the child-like affections which grow into learned attachment.

Our parents gave us the first gift, our life itself.

What makes a good parent? Someone who would teach, guide, sacrifice for, love unconditionally. Someone who shows how to seek balance, how to listen, how to respect others, how to connect to the world outside the home.

Good parents set their children free, knowing that the child will enter the world dressed in the teachings and ways of being they were given.

Wisdom, love, patience, joy, kindness, generosity, self-control, peace, faithfulness, humility. These ways of being were described by Saint Paul in his Letter to the Galatians (5). These are the ten Gifts of Love. They have to be taught, shown, and demonstrated. Some don't come naturally.

There is a problem however. These gifts are really heard to live. No parent is perfect. No Saint is perfect. No one said it was easy. The Family is the laboratory for the production of the final product … a good human being.

Parents need help. Mothers, fathers and siblings, aunts, uncles, grand-parents, cousins all need one another to survive a tumultuous world.

Ancient peoples, native to the land and proud of their ways understood this. They saw how brief and precarious life was and the Elders, the Prophets and clan leaders taught their people that survival required actions that reflected truth and reality.

Families learned wisdom and daily ritual through experience. From those early days, thousands of years ago certain truth were claimed, accepted and honored. They knew life was brief and the family was the testament of a group or culture which would live on far beyond the years of a human lifespan.

Parenting, family and homelife are the places where the ten gifts of love can happen.

A good mother doesn't make a man. She makes a boy. A good wife makes a man. A good father knows he ultimately must let his child go into the world without him and so he must show his love for his children as a steadfast beacon they will always see.

A good husband is a life-partner, a man who understands and travels the road of family life with his wife.

A good child will learn as the years go by that they do not have the right to possess their parents. A good sibling will honor and protect their siblings. These truths are the connectors, the fibers of family life, which allow humans to survive and flourish.

Wisdom ... Love ... Patience ... Joy ... Kindness ... Generosity ... Self-control ... Peace ... Faithfulness ... Humility ....

Brief lives on this earth. Hopefully eternal life afterwards. So much to learn. Family and home, caregiving and love.

CHAPTER 18

A Calling, Caring, and the Candles

*T*he word "calling" has multiple meanings. Its origins are multiple as well. The ancient Latin word for call is "vocare." In the Middle English era (1205 – 1250), call meant to "shout out" and may have come from Old Norse "Kallal" meaning to call out or Middle Dutch "Kallen" to herald.

Like most words we speak, "call" can be a noun, a verb, or an adjective. Its current use in my life is as a noun, "a calling" or a summons, a need, an awakening, a bringing to memory, a special fitness for work or a career, or a divine call to God's Service.

In the wonderful world of words where all human life resides, connections exist to other words, which become a woven net of truths.

"Vocare" was known in the 1400s as 'vocacio,' meaning to summon. It grew in use and therefore in meaning in the medieval world. In the 1500s we see its use in the word "vocabulary." Then it meant a word or term or the name of something being spoken, but now we see it in the word "vocation."

So … we are "called to a vocation …."

Another deep and beautiful word in our lives is the word "care." In ancient Latin, the word "cura" is the root word. It means to cure pain, concern, treatment, worry, diligence, solicitude. Depending on its usage, it is also a noun, a verb, or an adjective.

As the centuries passed before 900 AD "caru" became "chara", meaning to lament. In our day, we use the word "care" much like our ancient families did. Today "to care" means to show regard or desire, to protect, watch over, be vigilant and cautious, and to feel affection and love for something or someone.

A calling, a vocation, a caring—it is no coincidence that for many people a life of service to others means that service is given with love. A life of caregiving, in any form, is love trying to comfort and heal in any way possible.

Caring for others requires compassion, commitment and empathy and some of us put our needs aside to care for others. It's a natural gift for some people, but sometimes it is really hard to do.

Caring for others requires true self-scrutiny. It's not easy to put the needs of others before our own. Employed caregivers, nurses, doctors, aides, or anyone in the health profession or the many professions that attend to humanity have experienced moments when they are angry, frustrated, depressed, anxious or sad when they are helping others. They have to continually reinforce in their hearts and minds the facts.

The facts: Caregiving is a holy act and every time we give of ourselves to another, we are reinforcing our own inner life.

The small details always matter in a "calling," a "vocation," or a "caring" act. In my own life, I have many meanings inside those words, as I am sure you do as well. I also have the characteristic personality traits helpful to someone in the helping professions.

I am vigilant. I am careful with my hands. I use my hands in many healing and nurturing ways. I love order and having things in their "right place." I watch everything in my domestic life with attention to detail. I know how to keep things running smoothly. I never run out of essentials for my jobs, tasks or duties.

I love doing simple chores of housekeeping and cooking. Doing quiet contemplative activities in my home gives me comfort and purpose.

I love touching the objects I love—the smooth side of a stone, a soft feather, a down comforter.

I am a volunteer personality. If I see someone in trouble or needing assistance, I don't think twice before acting. I don't think of myself more than the other person, because I have learned the hard way, repeatedly I might add, that service, caring and love *never* let you come first.

When I began my nurse's training I had a strong calling to help others. I had been an English major in college and decided that as much as I loved to read, think, write and teach, I loved to act and help others more.

My kind of energy is suited for caregiving. My spiritual self has a voice inside me always giving me comfort and guidance as I help others.

Nursing is an astounding profession. My years as a surgical nurse highlight what I have described as the vigilant, watchful part of caring. Surgical nurses perform highly detailed, technically demanding acts during surgery.

They anticipate every move the surgeon makes. They prepare instruments, sutures, or bandages as they are called for. They pay amazing attention to the smallest detail.

I have memories of cases and patients I worked on that will never leave me. I am grateful I was able to be there, unseen to them to help them.

As I grew in my professional life the years passed. As a Nurse-Practitioner, a Director of Nursing, a Health Educator, a grant-writer, and a company owner, I always had the health, safety, and welfare of others as my guiding star.

Carefully navigating the connecting worlds of professional life, marriage and a daughter's love and devotion to her aging parents, I never resented one single act I performed in those moving spheres. I will always thank God and the prayers I sent to him over the years for blessing me with the flame within me to be a good person to others.

I recently was approached by a woman in my church who is in charge of "The Altar Guide." Episcopalian practice requires very specific procedures and rituals. Like any formal religion there is a time and a place for everything. Certain roles, duties, and physical realities make the church function smoothly.

Just like in the operating room, serving the patient and the surgeon, or in the hospice, giving solace to a family, or in my kitchen, placing daily instruments at a table or near a stove, serving the church in the Altar Guild requires devotion, vigilance, affection, caring and humility.

An altar is a sacred place within a sacred church. There are absolute requirements expected of me as I volunteer my time setting out specific items in their specific and allotted places.

It's a lot to learn. I look at the setup and cleanup lists, and try to memorize the Latin names given to little bottles, chalices, linens, water basins and candles. I watch carefully as the other women in the Altar Guild show me what to do. Many of these are like me—they have the caring, vocational, vigilant, detail-oriented, homemaker, good-wife-and-mother-and-daughter personalities. They are cheerful, happy, peaceful women and I feel honored they asked me to join them.

One day I was shown how to fill the candle containers in the prayer bench at the side of the altar. For years I have lit candles before Mass and pray to my parents, catching them up on the latest news.

Sometimes the candlewick wouldn't take the match. I would try another row or another candle in the same row. Once I even brought my own matches because there were none.

Now I'm filling the little cups each Saturday I'm assigned duty.

"Not too full, Nancy," my friend cautions me, "If you fill them too much, they won't light."

Like everything else in life, in our brief flame of life here, in our world of words and meanings, of vocations, of caring for others, candles need special attention too!

Next are the prayers we pray together before we start our Altar Guild duties, and an Italian prayer that I have in my kitchen, as in my Mother's kitchen for years.

> O Loving Savior, we pray you send your blessing upon this Altar Guild and the work of all its members; give us your grace that we may be loyal to your Holy Church, and faithful in our care of holy things. Grant that as we adorn and make ready your Altar we may learn greater love and reverence for all that belongs to your service, and through all outward symbols come to a clearer vision of the inward and spiritual truth taught by them. We ask in your name, blessed Lord and Master, Jesus Christ. AMEN.

> Most gracious Father who has called me your child to serve in the preparation of Your Altar, so that it may be a suitable place for the offering of Your Body and Blood, sanctify my life and consecrate my hands so that I may worthily handle those sacred Gifts which are being offered to You. As I handle holy things, grant that my whole life may be illuminated and bless You, in whose honor I prepare them, and grant that the people who shall be blessed by their use, may find their lives drawn closer to Him Whose Body and Blood is our hope and our strength, Jesus Christ our Lord. AMEN.
>
> *National Altar Guild Assoc.*

"Casa Mia, Casa Mia, per piccino che tu sia, tu mi sembri una bodia."

"My house my house, as little one you are, you are to me an abbey."

CHAPTER 19

Relationship

- Relationships are connections.
- Humans see things, places and people through their own eyes, hearts and minds.
- To relate with anything at all, animate or not, we must learn about them, what and who they are and introduce ourselves to them to learn their terms and identities.
- Compromise, awareness, and respect lead to successful intimate relationship.

Respect others' boundaries.

Respect the natural world and the natural order of all things.

- How do you get inside someone else's world?

Keep your own space, be aware and keep an open mind when you are close to someone

Learn to listen.

Accept other viewpoints.

Approach everyone and all things with love.

- Give your heart in your relationships.
- Soulmates have an intimate, secret connection.
- Our smiles are our gifts to others and God's gift to us.
- I can be myself "near" some people but not "with" some people.
- Some people are so toxic they should have a "CAUTION – POISON" label on them.
- When I am by myself I am in good company.
- Live each moment in grace and give everyone a loving space.
- Let me make today the most fully alive day I have ever known!
- Think of every hug and kiss you receive from a loved one as a deposit in your external savings account.
- Relationships have fronts and backs, visible and not seen places like the back of an art work. There is visible work in the painting and here are hidden details and information in the frame behind the glory of the artist.

There is no unity without relationship to others.

You can't chase affection. It doesn't work that way.

When you love someone, they become your second self.

- We live our lives alone in the company of others.
- "There is always some part of everything into every other thing. Even the most extreme opposites have some qualities in common."

Plato

- "All things can be alike or unlike."

Plato

- "When two go together, one always sees before the other. All men with companions are readier in thought, deed and word."

Homer

♥

CHAPTER 20

Connections

- World maps show where continents once were and their edges are a big jigsaw puzzle. The great masses of land once touched one another.
- All of life, nature, and the physical world are connected.
- Spider webs are connectors.
- The World Wide Web and social media are connectors.
- Connections can conceal interior truths and identities.
- Connections can start mysteries.
- Relationships are connections.
- Meeting others, seeing things on their terms and showing them your terms is a great connector.
- Compromise, awareness, respect, listening, putting others first will lead to intimacy and connection.
- The strange can become familiar. Familiar can become strange.
- Connections to others, to love and nature are our essential gifts as humans.

Connections

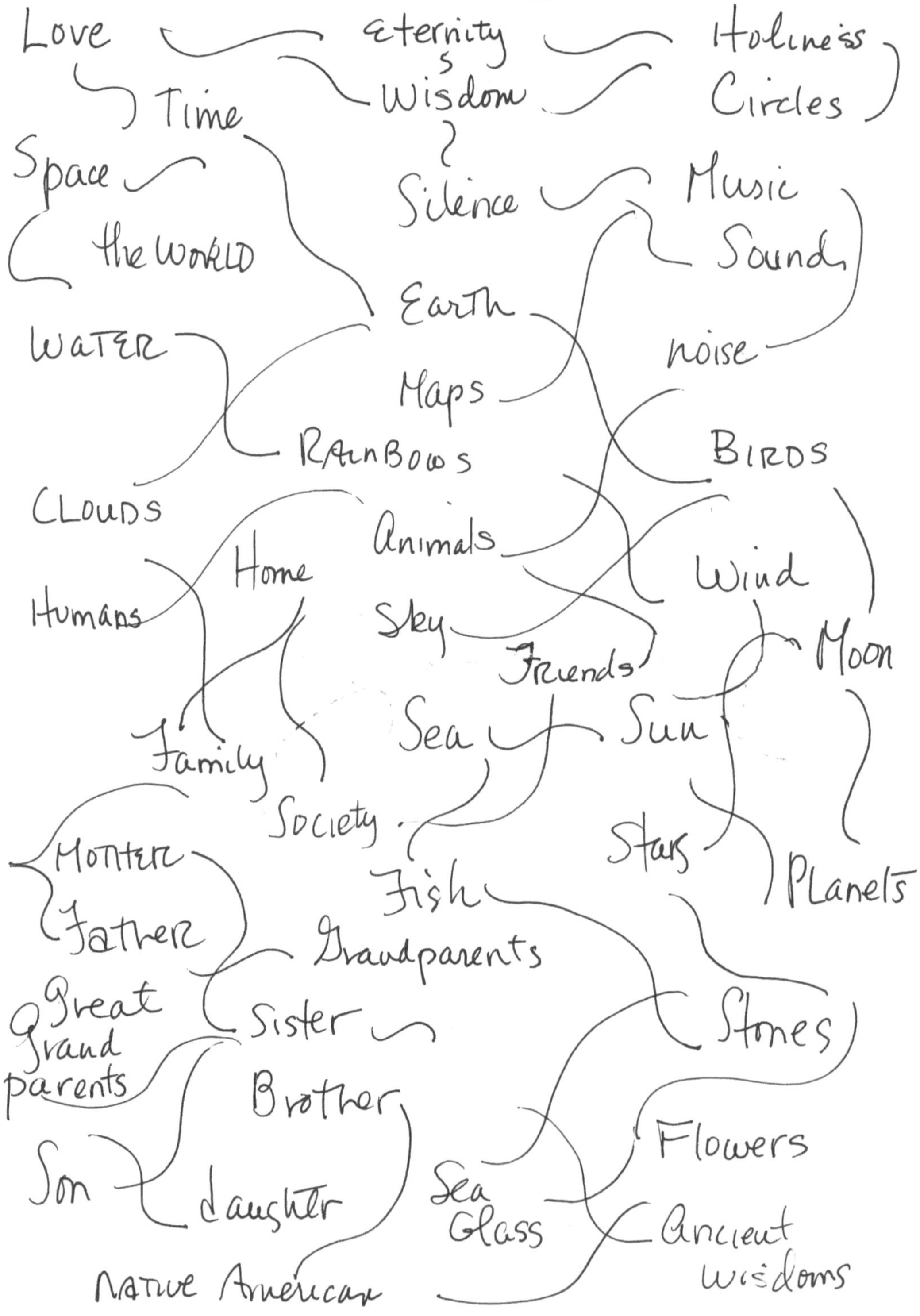

Love

Eternity
s
Wisdom

Holiness

Time

Circles

Space

Silence

Music

the WORLD

Sound

WATER

Earth

noise

Maps

CLOUDS

RAINBOWS

BIRDS

Animals

Wind

Humans

Home

Sky

Moon

Friends

Family

Sea

Sun

Society

Stars

Planets

MOTHER

Fish

Father

Grandparents

Great
Grand
parents

Sister

Stones

Brother

Son

daughter

Flowers

Sea
Glass

Ancient
wisdoms

NATIVE American

CHAPTER 21

Opposites

- What is an opposite? Is a question also an answer? Are there degrees of opposition (like adjacent angles in geometry)?
- Are relationships between people and living things always in juxtaposition?
- Is the opposite inside its opposer like a baby in its mother's womb or an acorn beside an oak tree?
- An opposite can instantly occur (life ⟶ death).

Darkness to dawn.

Death to Life inside death as an afterlife.

- An opposite can live inside another and that one inside yet another.
- The Roman God Janus had a temple. The temple ran East (day begins) and west (day ends). In the temple was a two-faced statue, one old, one young. Inscribed inside the temple were these words:

> Life = grief and joy on Earth
> Life = only joy and no grief in Heaven
> Life = no joy, only grief in Hell.

- In the fifth century BC (475), Heraclitus, a Greek wrote, "There is a natural harmonious balance between opposite powers and opposite processes. This balance is the source of the preservation of the Universe."

Ancient Taoism has yin/yang, male/female.

The ancient Gnostics believed in dualism, the symmetry of opposites – discord resolves to harmony.

- The reconciliation of opposites brings balance to someone facing old age or death.
- Plato and Socrates both wrote of the nature of opposites:

Plato said, "Spring follows winter in a never-ending rhythm, hence life must follow death."

Socrates believed that opposites emerge from opposites. "There is always some part of everything into every other thing. Even the most extreme opposites have some quality in common."

- All things are connected.

Opposites

east	west	black	white
north	south	heavy	light
man	woman	winter	summer
sunrise	sunset	spring	fall
moon	sun	concave	convex
up	down	stright	curved
holiness	sinfulness	wide	narrow
sweet	sour	weak	strong
light	dark	empty	full
tall	short	earth	sky
noise	quiet	wet	dry
happy	sad	unite	divide
short	long	speak	be slient
beautiful	ugly	ascetic	wordly
rich	poor	fertile	barren
near	far	war	peace
wise	foolish	life	death
cautious	impulsive	mortal	immortal
shy	outgoing	lost	found
truth	lies	symmetry	asymmetry
hard	soft	interior	exterior

Prayer of St. Frances of Assisi

Lord, make me an instrument of thy peace.
Where there is hatred, let me sow love.
Where there is injury, Pardon.
Where there is doubt, faith
Where there is despair, hope.
Where there is darkness, light.
Where there is sadness, joy.

O, Divine Master, grant that I may <u>not</u> seek
   To be consoled as to console.
   To be understood as to understand.
   To be loved as to love.
For it is in the giving that we receive.
   It is in the pardoning that we are pardoned.
   It is in the dying that we are born
   To eternal life.

- Opposites don't separate things. They connect things. The world is made up of opposing forces.
- The world is not predictable, chaos and balance are always present.
- Things are lost. Things are found.
- Things are given away. Things are received.
- Finders, keepers, losers, weepers.
- Things are remembered. Things are forgotten.

Things We Forget

- People from our past
- Our grandmother's recipes
- Doctors' appointments
- TV channel listings
- Names of people newly met
- Episodes of our college years
- To turn on our turn signals when driving
- Landmarks of our hometown
- Our country's history, our native people
- Time
- We forget to hope
- We forget to pray
- Our friends
- Birthdays
- Promises made
- Time again
- I have held many things in my hands and I have lost them all; but whatever I have placed in God's hands, I still possess.

Martin Luther King

- Nothing has changed the nature of man so much as the loss of silence.

Max Picard

- New: "There is always a gift on the other side of surrender."
- New: "To feel joy you must know sorrow."

The Things We Give Away

- Good deeds and acts of kindness
- Time
- Effort
- Old stuff, new stuff
- Opinions
- Coins to Salvation Army ringers
- Charity
- Our music, our art, our creations
- Examples of behavior, good or bad
- Second chances to others, forgiveness
- Time

The Things We Find

- Lucky pennies (angels send them)
- Orange-red maple leaves in autumn
- Lost wallets and keys
- People on Facebook
- Our identities
- Love
- New places to travel
- Peace inside our home
- Rainbows after rain
- Friends among fellow travelers
- Good mid-week airfares
- New authors
- Seashells and lucky stones
- Ideas that work
- Excellent hickory walking sticks
- Self-awareness in quiet contemplation
- Acceptance
- Changes in our aging
- Cool things at Goodwill and Salvation Army
- Books at the free library
- New recipes
- New ways to talk to friends and loved ones
- Time

The Things We Throw Away

- Old letters
- Old receipts
- Friendships
- Uneaten food
- Opportunities
- Health
- Junk mail
- Ideas that don't work
- Clothes that don't fit anymore
- Our children's baby things when they marry
- People who annoy us
- Opportunities
- Hopefully our angers and resentments
- Love
- Fallen twigs and dead roses
- Plastic and cardboard
- Old magazines
- Realtor advertisements
- Dull needles
- Time

Things We Lose

- Patience
- Sense of humor
- Socks in the dryer
- Coins in our pockets
- Health
- Our dreams
- Our money
- Our loved ones
- Millions of cells in our body every day
- Jobs
- Elections
- Football and baseball championships
- Opportunities
- Track of time
- Our hearing

- Our new routes while driving
- Car keys
- Our memories
- Our wisdom teeth and sometimes other teeth
- Our innocence
- Love
- Dreams of our youth
- Our freedom
- Time

Things We Keep

- Our genetic structure, our DNA
- Our personalities throughout our life
- Old photos
- Our child's first baby shoes
- Our Social Security number
- Our prejudices
- Hopes and dreams
- Our shoe size
- Hats, scarves, and mittens for cold places
- Bathing suits and suntan lotion for hot places
- Our cultural heritage
- Hope for a better world
- Whatever makes us feel secure
- Jewelry
- Favorite books
- Special art work
- Bicycles
- Old friendships
- New friendships
- Our promises
- Track of *time*

♥

CHAPTER 22

Love

- Is Love shapeless?
- Is Love Invisible?
- Does Love awaken at birth in humans and animals?
- Is Love timeless? Does Love need Time?
- Is Time loveless? Does time need Love?
- Is Love an internal or external force?
- Love and Faith are two different things.
- Love is too often categorized as an emotion. It is so much more than that.
- Love has proxies:
  - Grace
  - Patience
  - Generosity
  - Tolerance
  - Joy
  - Humor
  - Gentleness
  - Truthful actions, words, music
- Where does Love come from?
- Does Love ever disappear? Or does it gently recede as it teaches its lessons?
- All sensate creatures are hard-wired for Love.
- The human race often uses Love as a language.
- Love is an unsolvable mystery with really hard clues.
- Love is never a coincidence.
- Is Hate the only opposite of Love?
- Love uses signals and sends messages in many shapes and sizes.
- Love is the great connector.
- Love seeks to comfort and heal in any way possible.
- Nothing can separate me from Love if Love is not what I have, but what I am.
- Love is a unifier, a gift from the universe.
- We are only stewards of Love; it stays within us and passes to others.
- Love is not money or materials things.
- Love is not silent, but it may be quiet.
- Love is an action verb.

- Love is complicated yet simple, hard work yet joyful.
- We didn't invent Love (sorry Hallmark). Love invented us.
- Love always brings peace.
- Love yourself.
- Accept Love from others.'
- "One sees clearly only with the heart. Anything essential is invisible to the eyes."

Antoine de Saint-Exupéry

- Love isn't always touching skin to skin or being close. Often the lover is far away from the loved.
- Love never gives up. Wisdom does not grow weary. Love and wisdom go together.
- Sometimes we love someone who want to be loved, to be seen, and to see, but doesn't' want to be close. When that happens to you, look and wave, smile and blow kisses from your heart through the distance created.
- Self-love is not vanity
- Anger is ugly; Love is beautiful.
- Love doesn't' leave; it stays.
- Love is not martyrdom.
- Love yourself first, everything will follow.
- Always stay near to what you love.
- Love and self-control purify the soul.
- Love is the measure of our ability to bear crosses great or small.

♥

CHAPTER 23

It Is Vast and Eternal and into It You Must Fly

Are you afraid of death? Are you afraid of dying? Have you thought about Eternity? Do you feel the connections between Life and Death? Have you lost a loved one to a painful illness that led to Death?

Like all profound realities I have asked questions about Death. I am not afraid to die. That much I have known inside my deepest self for years.

I'm more curious and excited about Eternity because I know there are amazing mysteries awaiting me. In what form or language or mystical apparatus I haven't a clue. But I do know how brief a moment my Life on this Earth is and I feel that my soul, my spirit, and actions, my prayers, and my love for others is my passageway to the Unknown.

I would comfort some of my dying patients or grieving loved ones with a simple statement given with a close hug, "Every time someone dies a baby is born somewhere and the circle of life goes on."

I truly believe that my soul will live in the Forever. I don't even know what to call "after-death." Is it Eternity? Is it the Great Beyond? Is it Heaven? Is it simply a Great Sleeping?

I have read Greek philosophers, great ancient mysteries, Native holy men, church doctrine, Confucius, Mohammed, poets, and great writers to see if I can learn more than I already accept about Death.

I admire the wisdom, I am humbled by the clarity, and I am intrigued by the assessments of humans throughout the centuries as to what Death actually is.

It seems to me that Death is the end of a life here on Earth, which is lived in preparation for a great mysterious journey.

I know that illness, accidents and untimely ends to life are often painful and crushing to the survivors who have to live with the emptiness that a human leaves behind.

I don't want to have a painful death. I don't want to die before my husband or loved ones. I want to live the best life I can. I want to stay healthy and happy in a graceful and simple longevity.

I have always felt that if I can live a humble life, loving others, seeking simple truths, being a good person connected to the creation of this world, then I cannot fear Death. Why? Because I'm preparing myself to enter a Great Mystery and begin a Great Journey.

Facing Death

In ancient times, Death seemed closer and maybe that is why so many writers described the connecting fibers of human life to what could come afterwards.

- In ancient Japan, Samurai warriors, trained in philosophy as well as martial arts, were taught that Death was an honor:

    Samurai believed to bear and face all calamities and adversities with patience and a pure conscience.

- Meniscus, a Chinese philosopher of the fourth century before Christ, wrote:

    When Heaven is about to confer a great office on anyone, it first exercises his mind with suffering and true Honor. Death lies in fulfilling Heaven's desire.

- Socrates, Greek philosopher of the fifth century before Christ, wrote:

    Do not fear Death—a great mystery lies ahead, a journey of the Soul. If you live Life well, with justice, virtue, courage, honesty, kindness, respect for family and country, you are prepared for a good Death.

- The French Philosopher Montaigne wrote in the sixteenth century:

    Meet Death with dignity. Go out of this world as you entered it. You entered life through a passage without feeling or fright. Make it again through this same passage from Life to Death. Your death is part of the order of the Universe, a part of the life of the world. We borrow our lives from each other. Men, like runners, pass along the torch of Life.

- Chief Seattle of the Puget Sound Duwan-ush tribe said in the nineteenth century one profound sentence:

    There is no death, only a change of worlds.

I have always sensed these sayings and approaches to Death as the real reason I am alive. I've always sensed that we are connected to unseen and unknown energies that are timeless. I can call it, "Soul." I connect Soul to Grace, and connect Grace to Hope, and then connect Hope to Love.

To me, Death is not a dark empty place. That is why I'm not afraid. Not a day goes by when I don't talk to my beloved parents. Both met their deaths with courage and humility. I still am their daughter, giving them daily updates on family and events. We are still connected in life beyond the physical. Whatever we were to each other, we are that still. They are out of sight only, never out of mind.

I am comforted by grace, the quiet prayers of my heart, sometimes not spoken with words but with great quiet swaths of peace, images and sensations. I feel that my spirit, my very human essence, is connected by grace to places beyond my body.

I don't know if that is Soul or Spirit, Hope or Mystery. It doesn't matter. I am comfortable that I will live someday beyond my body and I too will talk to loved ones and them to me. Our Love is Eternal.

I believe that after my physical body is gone, I will exist in a placed where my emotions or behaviors won't matter. I will not be burdened by constraints, obligations, or responsibilities. I believe I will be part of a Great Mystery, a Great Truth, and I won't needs words.

My life has always been a prayer. My belief in a force larger than life calls this force "God." It is for me the best way to connect to this Spirit. I have a relationship with God as he listens to my soul speak.

I have known the compass points of Heaven. As in ancient times, I see God above me, below me, to the left of me, and to the right of me. Love is my compass, so I know that Death is a continuation of this life force, God, which is Love, and so I will always be smiling.

So, Death is a higher Power, an essential Divinity? Grace, Hope, Love, Wisdom all bring me to this place. I will never be alone, ever. It's going to be amazing.

CHAPTER 24

I Am Here, Where Are You?

*T*he ancient Greek word "mysterion" meant "secret worship." Centuries later, the Latin word "mysterium" meant "mystery, something that cannot be rationally explained."

"Mysticism" takes the root "myst" of both words and means "the use of intuitive knowledge or meditation, or asceticism, allowing a direct union with God or some ultimate reality."

As I search for meaning in my life and the "Beyond," I know only that mysteries have many facets. Like a large diamond, Spirit and Grace and Wisdom and Life Eternal shine from a mystery beckoning me always towards its light.

Because the world I live in is chaotic, turbulent, and unpredictable, I am aware that the mystery I seek does not have an easy solution or a quick answer. I know I will be seeking to balance my darkness with light, my disorder with order, my goodness with badness, because I won't be eligible to find mystery, if I don't live in Grace.

I know I am connected to the Universe and that my life is brief. Without being mentored in this search, I have sought my own instruction.

I know that an unconditional acceptance of Divinity is an absolute requirement. I know that I must be vigilant and always seek Truth. The ancient Latins used the word "vigilare," which meant "to keep awake." My vigilance is my awareness and alertness and acceptance of a life of the Spirit, not visible in my daily activities, but always beneath the surface the light shines for me.

I know that I need to be still and quiet in the moments I use to search carefully for Truths.

I know that mysteries are not evident, but like to stay hidden. It's as though a seeker such as myself has to show that I know how to live (how to pray, how to love, how to touch others, how to seek peace in nature and relationships), before I can qualify as an acceptable candidate for exposure to mystery.

I know I have to pray, be mindful and allow my soul to see what is beyond. I certainly understand why contemplatives throughout man's centuries on earth have sought quiet solitude and stillness.

I'm smiling as I write this, but I also am shaking my head with ironic amusement at what I am going to say next.

How can a lifetime of wonder, curiosity, yearning, passion and certainty for searching for mystery be written in a list? Why not? My inner voice says, "Why not?"

1. Always speak from your heart with sincerity and you will influence others because speaking from your heart brings your spirituality to the surface.
2. Be disciplined in your daily routines.
3. Balance your pursuits for happiness with acts of responsibility.

4. Be at ease with solitude.

5. Pray when you do physical things so rhythm governs like a mantra.

6. Take care of those you love.

7. Find comfort in your home.

8. Live a simple, elegant, quiet life.

9. Touch flowers, plants and nature often

10. Humble yourself enough to be vital, but not self-important.

11. Allow yourself to see deep inside yourself.

12. Smile a lot and laugh a lot.

13. Be artistic in any way you can.

14. Pray to the outside of yourself.

15. Embrace aging which can hug back with wisdom.

16 Always ask why? Where? How? When? Be inquisitive.

17. Watch everything around you.

18. Don't worry about what others think. Listen to your own counsel.

19. Always strive for humility.

20. Always follow true North—that's where mystery is.

Conclusion

*T*here are many layers of history and sources of information in the essays and stories you have just read. Experience, like knowledge, can't always be documented or given an ISBN number. My bibliography is therefore a very minimal one.

Just as it took years of wondering and watching my world for me to collect quotes and authors, I am sure you also have your own sources, your own teachers, your own stories—your own years.

What are your stories? What language do you speak and how do you speak it?

What is your gift? Where does your heart lead you? Where do you find your meaning? What are your clues?

What are your mysteries?

Like rivers stones beneath a running stream, we touch and connect to our world.

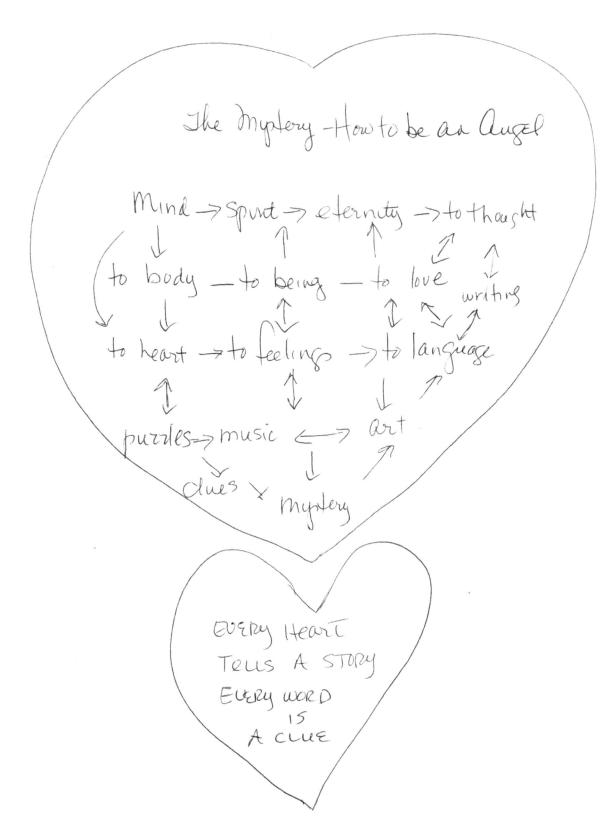

The Mystery - How to be an Angel

Mind → Spirit → eternity → to thought
  ↓   ↑   ↑   ↗   ↑
to body — to being — to love   writing
  ↓   ↓   ↑   ↑   ↘   ↗
to heart → to feelings → to language
  ↑   ↑   ↓   ↗
puzzles → music ⟷ art
    ↘   ↓   ↗
  clues × mystery

EVERY HEART
TELLS A STORY
EVERY WORD
IS
A CLUE

THE STORY, THE MYSTERY

Across

2. a present, donation, a talent
7. winged flutter-flying bright colored insect
8. enduring without complaint
9. goodness and gentleness
11. to wish, desire or want
13. binding rule of conduct and procedure
14. wrath, strong displeasure
16. being alone, seperate from others, seclusion
17. things or people joined together
18. female force of the universe (Chinese)
20. the end of life
22. the act or result of thinking, ideation or conception
23. something that cannot be explained, a secret
24. a state of equilibrium
25. receiving with good grace
28. a problem, activity or game requiring ingenuity to solve
30. animating principle of life an energy in mankind
32. freedom from hypocrisy
33. a heavenly spiritual being
36. sounds, tones and rhythms in composition
37. kinship or association
39. courage, bravery, heroism, self-sacrifice
41. past , present and future in continum and dimension
44. an ailment, sickness, state of being in poor health
46. the supreme being, creator of the universe
48. adherence to the truth, facts and law
49. te entire structure of a person, animal or entity
50. group connected by heritage, name or culture
52. a piece of hewn or shaped rock
53. enormous body of salt water
57. high regard or respect
58. to the end of time
59. the essential liquid of all life
61. a mass of visible vapor and shape in the sky
62. male force of the Universe (Chinese)
63. strong tender affection
64. feathered creatures, most who fly

Down

1. a quality of being seen and/or sensed
2. mild, soft serenity
3. gracious giving to others
4. on the other side of something
5. deep meditative form of Buddhism
6. brief life-lesson story often using animals as actors
10. fact or fiction, a narrative
12. spectral arch of light in the sky
15. the granting of pardon
16. calmness, silence, motionless quiet
19. the entire physical universe
21. artistic imaginative original skill
26. the creation of works in all genres
27. kowledge, insight, intuitionn
28. state of tranquility, absence of war
29. endless, limitless time
31. reality and fact
34. the vital state of growth, existence, reproduction
35. pleasure and joy
38. modesty, quiet simplicity
40. unconscious and conscious process in the human brain
42. a fact, idea or intuition that solves a puzzle or mystery
43. soundness and well-being of mind and body
45. gladness, gaiety, pleasure
47. orbiting body around the sun
49. the stae of existing
51. a radiant celestial object
54. for all time
55. a divine state of harmonious being
56. a unit of sound or writing with a definition and meaning
57. an amusing and comical quality
60. armed strife

THE STORY, THE MYSTERY

Across

2. a present, donation, a talent
7. winged flutter-flying bright colored insect
8. enduring without complaint
9. goodness and gentleness
11. to wish, desire or want
13. binding rule of conduct and procedure
14. wrath, strong displeasure
16. being alone, seperate from others, seclusion
17. things or people joined together
18. female force of the universe (Chinese)
20. the end of life
22. the act or result of thinking, ideation or conception
23. something that cannot be explained, a secret
24. a state of equilibrium
25. receiving with good grace
28. a problem, activity or game requiring ingenuity to solve
30. animating principle of life an energy in mankind
32. freedom from hypocrisy
33. a heavenly spiritual being
36. sounds, tones and rhythms in composition
37. kinship or association
39. courage, bravery, heroism, self-sacrifice
41. past , present and future in continum and dimension
44. an ailment, sickness, state of being in poor health
46. the supreme being, creator of the universe
48. adherence to the truth, facts and law
49. te entire structure of a person, animal or entity
50. group connected by heritage, name or culture
52. a piece of hewn or shaped rock
53. enormous body of salt water
57. high regard or respect
58. to the end of time
59. the essential liquid of all life
61. a mass of visible vapor and shape in the sky
62. male force of the Universe (Chinese)
63. strong tender affection
64. feathered creatures, most who fly

Down

1. a quality of being seen and/or sensed
2. mild, soft serenity
3. gracious giving to others
4. on the other side of something
5. deep meditative form of Buddhism
6. brief life-lesson story often using animals as actors
10. fact or fiction, a narrative
12. spectral arch of light in the sky
15. the granting of pardon
16. calmness, silence, motionless quiet
19. the entire physical universe
21. artistic imaginative original skill
26. the creation of works in all genres
27. kowledge, insight, intuitionn
28. state of tranquility, absence of war
29. endless, limitless time
31. reality and fact
34. the vital state of growth, existence, reproduction
35. pleasure and joy
38. modesty, quiet simplicity
40. unconscious and conscious process in the human brain
42. a fact, idea or intuition that solves a puzzle or mystery
43. soundness and well-being of mind and body
45. gladness, gaiety, pleasure
47. orbiting body around the sun
49. the stae of existing
51. a radiant celestial object
54. for all time
55. a divine state of harmonious being
56. a unit of sound or writing with a definition and meaning
57. an amusing and comical quality
60. armed strife

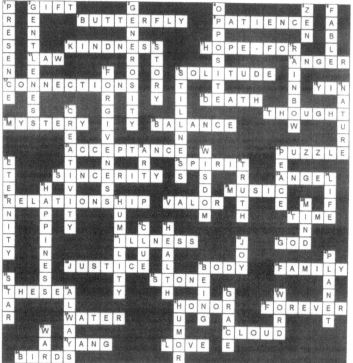

L
O
EVERY HEART
E   HAS   T
O
A   U
STORY   C
H
EVERY MYSTERY   N
O
HAS   W
D
A   SPIRIT
CLUE
P
Z
Z
L
E

Every
words
a clue

Love
Mystery
clues
words
hearts
touch
spirit

puzzles
Story

Bibliography

Deloria, Jr., Vine. *God Is Red.* Fulcrum Publishing, Wheat Ridge, Colorado, 1994. ISBN: 1-55591-176-5.

Inazo Nitobe. The Way of the Samurai. Arcturus Publishing, LTD. Canterbury, United Kingdom, 2011. ISBN: 978-84837-722-6.

Kimmerer, Robin Wall. *Braiding Sweetgrass: Indigenous Wisdom, Scientific Knowledge, and the Teachings of Plants.* Milkweed Editions, Minneapolis, Minnesota, 2013. ISBN: 978-1-57131-335-5.

McMurty, Larry. *Crazy Horse.* Weidenfeld & Nicolson, London, England, 1999. ISBN: 0297842803.

Neihardt, John G. & Black Elk. *Black Elk Speaks – Being the Life Story of a Holy Man of the Oglala Sioux.* University of Nebraska Press, Lincoln, Nebraska, 1932. ISBN: 0-8032-8359-8.

The New International Webster's Concise Dictionary of the English Language. Trident Press International, 1997. ISBN: 1-888777-09-5.

Sams, Jamie & Twyla Nitsch. *Other Council Fires Were Here Before Ours: A Classic Native American Creation Story as Retold by a Seneca Elder, Twylah Nitsch, and Her Granddaughter, Jamie Sams.* HarperOne, San Francisco, California, 1991. ISBN: 0-06-250763-x.

Shelley, Percy Bysshe. "The Cloud." https://www.poetryfoundation.org/poems/45117/the-cloud-56d2247bf4112.

Wikipedia, The Free Encyclopedia. Rainbow.

About the Author

Nancy Russo Wilson was born in New York City and came to Ithaca, New York as an infant. Her father was a surgeon as is her brother, several uncles and several cousins. Her aunts were nurses. She grew up listening to stories of healing. laced with Italian interpretations of life, love, food and family ... Nancy was one of the first five-hundred Nurse Practitioners trained in the United States. She graduated in 1976 and went into Family and Women's Health. Her many years of advanced Nursing practice include College Health, Family Health, Prison Health, Pain Management and Elder Care.

In addition to her Nursing degrees Nancy holds a BS degree in Health Education from SUNY Cortland College and a Masters of Industrial and Labor Relations from Cornell University.

Although she is officially retired, Nancy spends hours in helping others often spontaneously and with laughter.

Her passions are swimming, cooking and living a natural and simple life with her husband Bruce.

Nancy splits her time between Ithaca and the Finger lakes of New York and in Sarasota Florida.

CPSIA information can be obtained
at www.ICGtesting.com
Printed in the USA
JSHW040316310123
36928JS00002B/4